A Checklist of the
Letters of Richard Aldington

Compiled With an Introduction by

Norman Timmins Gates

SOUTHERN ILLINOIS UNIVERSITY PRESS
Carbondale and Edwardsville

Feffer & Simons, Inc.
London and Amsterdam

Library of Congress Cataloging in Publication Data

Gates, Norman T.
    A checklist of the letters of Richard Aldington.

    Includes indexes.
    1. Aldington, Richard, 1892-1962--Correspondence
--Bibliography. I. Title.
Z8025.4.G28 [PR6001.L4]   821'.9'12 [B]
ISBN 0-8093-0781-2   76-21638

For My Son
Norman Ernest Gates
Who Hears a Different Drummer

Contents

Contents

Preface

A checklist of letters, it seems to me, must always be
preliminary. By its very nature it is incomplete: if
its compilation were to await the opening of the last
trunk in someone's attic and the untangling of the last
estate enmeshed in law, its time of greatest usefulness
would have passed. The purpose of a listing of letters is
to provide a useful tool for anyone interested in studying
the man or woman who wrote them; thus, the checklist
should precede editions of letters, a biography, and even,
ideally, critical work. To wait for the final run of
letters to be uncovered and for it to be completed, would
result in a checklist that gathered dust on library shelves,
its hour having come and gone.

Checklists, therefore, encourage addenda, and their
compilers welcome those notes which distress other
authors by calling attention to their omissions. There are
doubtless many letters held by individuals who inevitably
escaped my nets of inquiry. Many letters whose existence I
am aware of were not available for listing. These are
mostly in the hands of individuals, some of whom have not
yet segregated their correspondence even though they have
preserved it. In some cases, however, collections of
Aldington's letters held by libraries are not available
for cataloguing because they are under legal restriction.
In those cases where letters were known to exist but could
not yet be listed, for whatever reason, or where the
possibility of letters was even suspected, note has been
made at the appropriate place in the Checklist so that
future researchers may investigate further.

Mailings to university and other large libraries
naturally provided the majority of the over seven thousand
listings that are included here. These represent
collections as large as the two thousand-odd letters at
Southern Illinois University and as small as one or two
letters which some faithful archivist reported. Librarians
were unfailingly generous in the assistance they gave in
indexing these holdings; in most cases, large collections
were catalogued or checked by the compiler or by local
scholars. Although most of these repositories are in the
United States, libraries in Australia, Canada, and Great
Britain hold Aldington letters. A considerable debt of
gratitude will always be owed by present and future scholars
to those men and women and their institutions who had the
foresight and the means to preserve these collections.

Understandably, those letters most difficult to account
for are the ones which remain in the hands of private
holders including original recipients. In his preface to
Imagism & the Imagist (1930) Glenn Hughes says, "It seems
inevitable, therefore, that no literary history can be
perfect, for the contemporary historian withholds facts
and the later one cannot discover them!" The problem that
the letter-checklist compiler faces is equally perplexing:
if he waits long enough his task will be easier because
almost all letters will have found their way into the
hands of libraries, but by that time his checklist will no
longer be urgently needed if, indeed, he is still around
to finish compiling it. Mailings were made to Aldington's
known friends, literary associates, publishers, and
family, as well as to scholars interested in him and his
first wife, H. D. Notices in literary journals in both
the United States and England were also used to call
attention to this work and to ask for assistance. The

response was generous and surprisingly rewarding: letters
were uncovered in places as far apart as Japan, Russia,
and Australia, and ranged in number from the almost
thousand held by the late Professor Norman Holmes Pearson
to a treasured few owned by admiring correspondents. I am
especially indebted to these many individual holders of
Aldington's letters who took the time and trouble to list
their holdings for me or who gave me access to them.

Ideally, this list would include every letter Aldington
wrote and would give complete descriptive data and a
synopsis of each letter's content. Even if the time for
such an undertaking were available (over five years have
elapsed since a beginning was made on this work), no
publisher could possibly justify the expense of producing
such an extensive book in the face of low potential demand,
today's inflated production costs, and sharply curtailed
university press subsidies. Obviously, compromises had to
be made. The first aspect of the ideal checklist to be
abandoned was the synopsis of the individual letters;
then, it was decided to combine into one entry all letters
of one kind and from one place to the same recipient. A
listing such as "195 - 3 March 1956 to 6 July 1962 - tls,
Sury, SIU" (indicating Aldington wrote to the recipient
under whose name the entry appears one hundred and ninety-
five typed, signed letters from Chez Alister Kershaw,
Maison Sallé, Sury-en-Vaux, Cher, France, between 3 March
1956 and 6 July 1962 and that these letters can be found
in the Morris Library of Southern Illinois University at
Carbondale) puts into one line data which would otherwise
require over ten printed pages. Despite such compromises
the Checklist and the following chapters which were derived
from it will it is hoped prove valuable tools to the
researcher who is interested in Aldington, his

correspondents, or his era.

Obviously I owe a debt of gratitude to each of the
individuals, firms, and libraries shown under the list of
"Repository Symbols" and to the individual recipient-
holders. All of these generously and willingly furnished
the data necessary for the completion of the Checklist,
or permitted examination of their holdings of Aldington
letters; many did both. Correspondence with them over the
past five years and their patient replies to many queries
attest to the extent to which they made this work possible.
It seems cold and formal to thank institutions when those
who helped were individuals, and it is difficult to single
out some without foregetting others. I do want to extend
personal thanks, however, to the staffs of the following
libraries and to those individual holders with whose
collections I worked at one time or another: Donald
Gallup, Peter Dzwonkoski, and the staff of the Beinecke
Library; the staff of the British Museum Library; the
staff of the Houghton Library; Warren Roberts, David
Farmer, Sally Leach, and the staff of the Humanities
Research Center; Kenneth Duckett, David Koch, Alan Cohn,
and Katharine Lockwood of the Morris Library; Thomas
Whitehead and the staff of Temple University Library;
and Professors Norman Holmes Pearson, Harry T. Moore, and
Selwyn Kittredge. I also owe thanks to the late Norman
Pearson and to Harry T. Moore for advice about the
preparation of this Checklist; and, in connection with the
writing of my Introduction, to Harry Moore for his various
introductions to Aldington's works, to Selwyn Kittredge
for the use of his unpublished work "The Literary Career
of Richard Aldington," and to Sidney Rosenthal whose
1967 Harvard University thesis "The Fiction of Richard
Aldington" and "Richard Aldington and the Excitement of

Reason" (in *Twenty-Seven to One...*, 1971) were helpful. I
am grateful to Mrs. Margery Lyon Gilbert for sharing her
childhood memories of her brother with me. A fresh
reading of Aldington's *Life For Life's Sake* and Kershaw
and Temple's *Richard Aldington: An Intimate Portrait* was
most useful. My colleague, Dr. Robert Winter, was kind
enough to read the manuscript of my Introduction and to
make helpful suggestions. I wish to thank Catherine
Aldington Guillaume and Alister Kershaw for permitting me
to quote briefly from Aldington's unpublished letters and
for the generous help they regularly gave me.

To Miriam J. Benkovitz, professor of English at Skidmore
College, who is a distinguished scholar of the modern
British period and has edited several runs of Aldington's
letters, including *A Passionate Prodigality: Letters to
Alan Bird from Richard Aldington, 1949-1962* (1975), I
owe profound thanks. It was she who first suggested the
need for this Checklist and did a great deal of
the preliminary planning for it; indeed, we originally
hoped to compile it together and only the heavy pressure of
her other commitments prevented our collaboration.
Nevertheless, Miriam Benkovitz has given me many
valuable suggestions, has read portions of my manuscript,
and, indeed, done everything possible to help me---I am
most grateful to her.

I also owe special thanks to all those who helped to
make this book, but especially to my editor, Beatrice R.
Moore, who quietly smoothed out many rough spots; to my
typist Meg Fitzsimmons whose painstaking work is reflected
on these pages; and, of course, to my wife, Gertrude, who
patiently read and reread this text so many times from the
first listings to the final version that I am sure she
never wants to see it again.

    And finally my thanks to the Rider College Faculty
Research Program for a Grant-in-Aid which covered some of
the travel expenses in connection with this work.

                              N. T. G.

Haddonfield, N.J.
10 August 1976

A Checklist of the Letters of Richard Aldington

1

Introduction

Richard Aldington, christened Edward Godfree Aldington,
was born at Portsea, Portsmouth, Hampshire, England, on
July 8, 1892, to Jesse May and Albert Edward Aldington.
His mother was a girl of Kentish peasant stock with a
strong will and an emotional nature; his father was a clerk
articled to a local solicitor. The Aldington family were
wealthy pre-Norman Conquest Saxon landowners who eventually
became yeoman farmers, millers, and lesser gentry. There
was a De Ricardo de Aldington in 1327. Harbington, the
historian of the time of James I, says of the family:
"Aldinton in Badsy, Worchestershire, gave the name to a
family as ancient heere as the Conquest, a streme once
greate, but now dispersed into lesser brookes. The male
line, the more it worketh the better it lyveth."

   When Aldington was still quite young his parents moved
to Dover, where he attended preparatory schools at Walmar
and St. Margret's Bay and later studied four years at Dover
College. As a boy Aldington did not like Dover, he tells
us in his poem "Childhood," but was happier when his family
moved into the country of the South Foreland, first for
summers and then year around. Both Aldington and his
sister Margery mention in their writings the pleasures of
the chalk-cliff beaches, prawning, hunting for fossils on
the cliffs, and endless summer days of sea-bathing. It was
here, too, that Aldington began collecting butterflies, a
pastime which he was to pursue as an adult in many parts
of the world. The great ships which passed by in the
English Channel, the fearful wrecks on Goodwin Sands he
saw through his telescope, the cross-Channel trips to

Calais and Brussels contributed to the wanderlust of his
future years.

A change in family affairs resulted in a move away from
the Channel coast when Aldington was about sixteen. For
a few months he lived in suburban Harrow where, used to
the spectacular beauty of the South Foreland, he was
desperately unhappy; a further move to Teddington and his
enrollment at University College, London, changed his
outlook quickly. In the first place, his new home was in
a less city-like area and was close to the Thames, Bushy
Park, and Hampton Court where the country boy who wrote
lovingly many years later of the long walks he took over
rural roads inland from St. Margret's Bay could enjoy the
more formal beauty of lawns, terraces, and gardens.
Besides, he was able to visit in comparative solitude the
fine buildings and art galleries of Hampton Court.

Aldington's study in his father's very fine library,
together with the eclectic education provided him by
Dudley Grey, an older friend of his youth in Dover who
was a world-traveler and classical scholar, may have
prepared him poorly for a formal education at University
College. In any event, he was displeased with both the
exterior appearance and the scholastic standards there,
although he had good things to say about many of the
professors he got to know--curiously, he objected to the
University being coeducational: "a mistake in practice
however desirable in theory." Whether this youthful
rebellion against organized learning would have been
overcome in time and Aldington would have fulfilled the
early promise of academic achievement some of his teachers
saw in him was to remain unknown. His father, never astute
in financial matters, met with a sudden loss which forced
his son's withdrawal from the University. Although

Aldington tried to minimize the value of the degree he lost and emphasize the freedom he felt, the fact remains that, despite his scholarship in later years, he often seems on the defensive because he lacked the official stamp of academic approval.

Long afterward Aldington saw a pleasing symbolism in his last walk from University College down Gower Street toward Bloomsbury, but at the time he was faced with some difficult alternatives. Without the necessary academic background, normal avenues open to a young man of his social rank were closed and he was forced to consider clerking in the city. A well-meaning friend recommended that he do this until he was thirty-five or forty and then retire to a life of literature. Young Aldington decided instead to see what he could do to earn his living as a writer and accepted the offer of an established newspaper sportswriter to share his rooms and to help the older man cover some of his assignments. Armed with letters of introduction from his friend to several newspaper editors, Aldington also tried to sell some of the poems he had been writing; to his surprise one editor bought several. He quickly decided that by devoting part of his time to reporting and continuing to sell a few poems here and there he could make a Spartan living; he turned his back on the City forever.

After a few months of this ascetic life Aldington was taken to a literary party, possibly at Mrs. Deighton (Brigit) Patmore's, and for the first time met the people of London's literary avant-garde such as Ford Madox Hueffer (later Ford), Harold Monro, W. B. Yeats, and Ezra Pound. Through Pound he soon met H. D., who had known the American poet when both lived in Philadelphia; the two young poets, Aldington and "Dooley," as he later called her

affectionately, were quickly attracted to each other and
found that they shared a fervent love of classical Greece
and its literature. Aldington went to Paris in the spring
of 1912--"Ezra and H. D. were there, so I didn't lack
companionship." A small monthly allowance from his parents
helped to offset the loss of his job with the newspaper
reporter and his income from the sale of poems and articles
to newspapers. As most men do, given the opportunity, he
fell in love with Paris that spring; he wrote a few poems
and made some translations, but most of his time was spent
seeing the city and living its special rhythm. He also
made the beginning of a lifelong friendship with the
philosopher Henry Slonimsky whom he always greatly admired
and placed as a personality alongside Yeats and Lawrence.

     When Aldington returned to London that summer, he was
offered a part-time job on the Garton Peace Foundation; he
accepted and was assigned the task of criticizing Admiral
Mahan's views of naval strategy. This occupation did not
last long, since Aldington quickly became disillusioned
with the Foundation's ideas, but other important
opportunities were opening to the young poet. Probably
in the fall of 1912, after Pound, H. D., and Aldington had
returned to London from Paris, Pound unveiled his school of
Imagism nominating Aldington, H. D., and himself as the
three original Imagists. By this time Pound was also in
touch with Harriet Monroe of the new *Poetry Magazine* of
Chicago and thus was instrumental in getting the early
poems of H. D. and Aldington printed there. The payment
for these and the promise of Orage, editor of the *New Age*,
to take a series of articles on Italy prompted the young
poet to buy a ticket for Rome.

     Aldington arrived in Rome in December intending to stay
for two months; he stayed seven and, besides Rome where he

spent most of his time, visited Naples, Capri, Florence, Venice, and elsewhere. H. D. was along and, looking back, Aldington remembered this first visit to Italy as "the good time" when they read Sophocles in Rome, Theocritus and the *Greek Anthology* in Capri. The youthful poet did much of his important early work there, and his shortage of money did nothing to mar the joy of being young, alive, and in love in Italy in spring.

By the time Aldington returned to London via Paris (where he was in July 1913), Ezra Pound had plans under way for the first Imagist anthology, *Des Imagistes*, although it would not be published until the next year in New York and London. In October, H. D. and Aldington were married. Shortly before, through Pound's influence, Aldington had become literary editor of *The New Freewoman*, soon to be renamed *The Egoist*. This post, which enabled him to promote Imagism and contemporary literature in general, did not prevent him from continuing to write poetry and contribute to other literary journals. In 1914 Amy Lowell came to London and, since Pound was now occupied with Vorticism, interested the Aldingtons in continuing the Imagist Anthologies under her aegis--three of these anthologies entitled *Some Imagist Poets* were published in 1915, 1916, and 1917. Also in 1915, Harold Monro's Poetry Bookshop published Aldington's first individual volume of poetry, *Images 1910-1915*, which was followed in 1916 by an American edition, *Images Old and New*, published by the Four Seas Company in Boston.

Hence Aldington was well along the road he had planned for himself that day when he left University College and walked toward Soho, but his career was soon to be disrupted by the Great War which began in the autumn of 1914--later he was to write that he never recovered from

these war years. In the first flush of patriotic fervor
Aldington tried to register as a volunteer, but was
rejected because of a hernia operation he had undergone
earlier. So, for the time being, he continued his literary
work, adding for a short while the task of secretary to
Ford Madox Hueffer. In September of 1915 the Aldingtons
moved to Devon with their friend John Cournos, renting a
cottage Cournos had located near his friends Carl Fallas
and J. M. Whitham. Fallas and Aldington were called up
in June of 1916 and managed to stay together even when
Aldington was sent to France that December.

Aldington fictionalized his wartime experiences in *Death
of a Hero;* they did not differ greatly from the average
Tommy's, but they were seen vividly through the eyes of a
poet. Although the novel was not written until much later,
Aldington did manage a considerable amount of writing while
a soldier, some of which, with H. D.'s help, was also
published during this time. Finally, however, the war
disrupted Aldington's marriage as well as his career;
during his leaves he was seeing not only H. D., but also
Cournos's friend Dorothy Yorke, or Arabella, as she was
called. Eventually the poet's love seemed to divide into
a spiritual union with H. D. and a physical one with
Arabella.

In February of 1919 Aldington returned from Belgium to
London where he stayed only a short time before leaving for
The Hermitage, a cottage in Berkshire, near Reading, which
D. H. Lawrence turned over to him when the Lawrences left
England after the war. Aldington moved there with
Arabella that autumn after he and H. D. reached the
mutual decision to live apart. Before he left London to
settle again in the placid countryside that recalled the
rural area inland from his boyhood home, Aldington was

able to make important literary connections that were to
provide for him for a decade. These included the
acceptance of poems and articles by the *English Review*,
the *Anglo-French Review*, *To-Day*, *The Sphere* and, most
important of all, the *Times Literary Supplement*, for
which he eventually was the regular reviewer of French
books. He also became, in 1921, assistant editor of
T. S. Eliot's newly established *Criterion*. Furthermore,
during this period Aldington was able to arrange for the
publication of five books of his poetry in England and
the United States.

The Berkshire years were for Aldington a period of
physical and mental rebuilding. Like almost all soldiers
who survived the war, he was left with serious aftereffects,
including those from gassing and shell-shock. The
peaceful English countryside of the Kennet helped to heal
war scars of mind and body although, as he has said
himself, Aldington never completely shook off his wartime
experiences. During this same time, since he took very
seriously his position as reviewer of French literature
for the *Times*, he polished and perfected his command of
modern and Old French and Italian and read widely in
these literatures. This intensive work--was Aldington
trying to make up the lost years at University College?
--resulted not only in two books of poetry and a great
amount of literary journalism (some of which was reprinted
in book form as *Literary Studies and Reviews* [1924] and
French Studies and Reviews [1926]), but also in more than
a dozen volumes of translation. The latter provided the
basis for a lifelong career in translation which
eventually produced some thirty titles in all.

During the 1920s Aldington established his position as an
important critic and enjoyed an influential friendship with

the greatest literary critic of the period, T. S. Eliot.
For all these years he remained close to his cottage,
visiting London only when necessary, and then usually to
see Bruce Richmond of the *Times Literary Supplement*. There
were trips to Italy, with stop-offs in Paris, in September
and October of 1922 and in the spring of 1924; surely
Aldington tried to recapture the experiences of his prewar
years there.

In 1926 Lawrence returned to Europe from America and
visited Aldington at Padworth; possibly their conversations
about contemporary England and Lawrence's descriptions
of his adventurous wanderings caused Aldington to take
another look at his own life. He probably came to the
conclusion that he had somewhere taken a wrong turn on the
way that led from University College so long ago. Possibly
he felt that his life at Malthouse Cottage (where he had
moved from The Hermitage nearby), his journalism, his
translations, and all of his efforts to fit himself into
the London literary élite constituted really the same
bonds of society that he had once cast off. In any event,
while he still kept his cottage and returned there
occasionally until 1928, by the spring of 1927 he was again
in Paris. He and Arabella lived part of that winter in
London, but this only served to strengthen his resolution
to leave England permanently. A handsome payment from
Crosby Gaige for the anthology *Fifty Romance Lyric Poems*
helped to implement this decision. According to John
Cournos, Aldington declared his intentions at a pub
gathering of the *New Criterion* group; this occasioned
considerable shock since it was generally believed that
Aldington was marked for the editorship of the *Times
Literary Supplement* on Bruce Richmond's retirement.

April of 1928 found Aldington and Arabella in Paris,

where they stayed through the summer. In September they
went to Italy and then by boat, via Marseille, to the
island of Port-Cros where Jean Paulhan, editor of the
Nouvelle Revue Française, had rented the *vigie* (an old
observation fortress), which he lent to Aldington for
October and November. There was sufficient room for him
to invite guests, so Aldington asked the Lawrences and
Brigit Patmore to join them. A number of things happened
on Port-Cros that dramatically affected the rest of
Aldington's life--the details have not been sorted out, if
they can ever be, but we know the results. The Lawrences
left in November when the weather turned too cold for
D. H.'s tubercular lungs; Aldington said good-bye to him
in Toulon and never saw him again since Lawrence was
dead in less than sixteen months. Arabella left alone
for Paris, while Aldington and Brigit Patmore returned to
Paris together, where they met frequently until the cold
of winter drove them south to Italy.

In his memoirs Richard Aldington speaks of 1928 as "a
year of activity and change, a watershed of a year which
set me moving in another direction." Not only did his
personal life change at Port-Cros, but also while he was
there he began to write the long book that had been
simmering in his head since the war--the novel that was
to become *Death of a Hero*, and that would launch him on
a new phase of his extensive literary career. Aldington
published seven novels between 1929 and 1939 and one more
after World War II. Several collections of short stories,
three long poems, four editions of his collected poems, and
miscellaneous literary journalism also belong to this
period.

During most of this time Aldington and Brigit Patmore
lived the life of adventurous wandering that Lawrence had

made sound so attractive when he visited Malthouse Cottage
in 1926. In early 1929 Aldington was in Rapallo with Yeats
and Pound; he returned to Paris in February, where he met
with Donald Friede, his American publisher, with whom he
left a copy of his unfinished novel. A few days later
Aldington received a cable expressing interest in the book,
urging its completion, and offering an advance. After
finishing the novel quickly, Aldington stayed in Paris
waiting for his proofs and then was off to the south of
France for the summer, finally settling in La Seyne near
Toulon from July to September. There he translated the
Alcestis and wrote the short stories that he collected in
Roads to Glory.

In September Aldington returned to Paris to await the
British reception of *Death of a Hero*; it was scheduled two
weeks after the American edition, which was already being
reprinted. The news from England was good, and that autumn
in Paris Aldington, not yet forty, tasted the success most
authors only dream of. Leaving Paris, Aldington first went
to Rome and Naples, then stayed some time at Amalfi before
going on to Palermo and Sorrento; he spent January and
February of 1930 in Tunisia and Algeria. During 1930
Aldington wrote his second novel, *The Colonel's Daughter*,
while living on the French Riviera, in Venice, and in
southern Italy.

If Aldington had a permanent address in the 1930s it was
the Villa Koeclin, Le Canadel, Var, France, but from here
he made long visits to Spain and Portugal or to Austria.
In 1934, after finishing the manuscript of his fourth novel,
Women Must Work, he decided to visit Vienna and Budapest,
partly in hope of collecting blocked royalty accruals
since by now his work was being published in translation
in Hungary, Czechoslovakia, Poland, and Russia. He shipped

a car from London to Lisbon, spent two months in Portugal,
Spain, and France before driving through Switzerland and
crossing into Austria early in June. An automobile
accident near Feldkirch in which his knee was broken
prevented Aldington from ever reaching Hungary. He
remained in Feldkirch until that September, part of the
time in the local hospital and the rest in the hamlet
of Fontanella.

When he was able to drive again, Aldington left for
France, intending to return to the French Riviera, but
increasingly unsettled conditions in Europe prompted him
to return to London for the winter. While there, he broke
his knee again; his convalescence gave him time to write
some essays and finish his long poem, *Life Quest*. While
Aldington was recovering from this second accident, his
wanderlust returned, and he left London in February on a
banana boat en route to Tobago where he stayed until May
of 1935--there he wrote nearly all of the essays contained
in *Artifex* and made an anthology of Lawrence's prose which
he called *The Spirit of Place*.

From Tobago Aldington booked passage to the United States
where he rented a house on the Connecticut River at Old
Lyme. Although Aldington says he now considered the United
States his "headquarters" and, indeed, did not leave it
for good until ten years later, "twice complications of
life took [him] back to Europe for rather long periods."
The first of these brought him back to London in October
of 1935, where he appears to have stayed until March; in
April he was in Portugal and Spain, and by June had
reached Austria where he stayed until early September to
complete his novel, *Very Heaven*. He was back on the
French Riviera the same month, returned to London in
October, and to New York on the S.S. *Normandie* in December.

The year 1937 was another important one in Richard
Aldington's life. He had fallen in love with Brigit
Patmore's daughter-in-law Netta, then Mrs. Michael
Patmore; when he returned to London from his short trip
to New York, the two left for Italy, where Richard had
traveled first with H. D. in 1912. Aldington and Netta
were in Le Canadel by April and stayed there until
October; Aldington had finished his last important poem,
The Crystal World, and was working on a novel, probably
Seven Against Reeves. It was necessary for Aldington to
come to London to try to resolve the matter of Netta's
divorce; he had already asked and received H. D.'s consent
to dissolve their marriage of twenty years. The legal
problems with the Patmore's were not settled; by December
the couple were back at the Villa Koeclin in Le Canadel
where they stayed until May.

After a visit to Switzerland, where Aldington wrote to
a friend about Heinemann's plans for a Uniform Edition of
his works (this was never completed because of the war),
he and Netta returned to London and were married on
Saturday, 25 June 1938. Their daughter, Catherine, was
born in Liphook, Hants.; they had taken a summer cottage,
and by September they were back at the Villa Koeclin.
Aldington had gotten past the immediate difficulty
occasioned by his legal problems with the Patmores, but
the arrangements required of him were to create problems
for the future.

The Aldingtons remained in Le Canadel until February of
1939, when they left France for New York City via London.
The war clouds which threatened in 1935 were now blacker,
and Aldington undoubtedly felt that the time had arrived to
take his new wife and daughter to the United States. The
British newspapers had also created quite a scandal about

the couple's respective divorces and subsequent marriage; indeed, Aldington was shunned by many of his old friends. In New York, however, Pascal Covici, the man who was a partner in the firm which published Aldington's first novel, *Death of a Hero*, remained loyal. Covici, now senior editor at the Viking Press, was instrumental in Aldington's selection of Viking as his new American publisher. The Aldington's lived in New York City for their first six weeks, then spent part of the summer in Rhode Island, where Aldington finished his novel *Rejected Guest* and, with Basil Dean, dramatized his *Seven Against Reeves*.

Returning to New York City in the autumn, Aldington found it difficult to obtain the kind of general literary work that had been available to him in London; he accepted several engagements for university lectures which did not, however, pay well. In June of 1940, Aldington returned to Old Lyme, Connecticut where he rented a house near the one he had lived in five years earlier. During this summer he sold the serial rights of his memoirs to the *Atlantic Monthly;* these were published during the next year by Viking with the title *Life For Life's Sake*--he was forty-eight when he wrote what he felt then was his farewell to Europe; indeed, it was a farewell to the prewar Europe he had known. Aldington was working hard on his memoirs that summer, and the first installment appeared in the September issue of the *Atlantic*, but even before this he had made an important literary commitment: he accepted the editorship of *The Viking Book of Poetry of the English-Speaking World*.

The idea for the Viking anthology grew out of a January conversation between Harold Guinzburg, Viking president, and Aldington. By spring, Aldington was using the Columbia

University Library near his apartment, and plans were
proceeding well; one of the reasons he moved again to Old
Lyme was to be near the Yale University Library. That fall
he felt that he had to work in the Library of Congress; he
stayed in Washington from November 1940 to February 1941.
By March 1 the work on the anthology was completed, and
the Aldingtons left for Florida; both Aldington and his
daughter had been ill with influenza, and doctors advised
a warmer climate for Catherine's recuperation. Before
they left Washington, Aldington's plans were to stay in
Florida until mid-April and then to spend the summer at
Frieda Lawrence's ranch in New Mexico.

Jamay Beach, Nokomis, on the west coast of Florida near
Sarasota, proved delightful to Aldington, possibly because
it reminded him of the Mediterranean coast of France
which he loved so much. He busied himself correcting the
proofs of his huge anthology and postponed his trip to New
Mexico until the end of May. The Aldingtons returned to
Florida in July, sooner than planned, because the altitude
of the Lawrence ranch made them ill. Although he did agree
with Lawrence, who wrote that the ranch was beautiful,
Aldington did not like the summer thunderstorms or the
"appalling diseases," and was bored by the society of Taos
which he called "a weary remnant of the Montparnasse
champagne bohemia." Aldington was glad to get back to his
peaceful Florida beach, and in January of the next year,
1942, began work on a biography of the Duke of Wellington
which was published in 1943. This was the first of the
important biographies that would constitute his major
literary work over the next decade.

In July of 1942, Aldington broke his stay at Nakomis by
taking a rail journey to a Writers' Conference held at the
University of Colorado in Boulder. By August, when he

returned, he had decided to move west to Hollywood because
of the chance for a screen-writing job there. He had
reason to be hopeful, since he had sold the film rights
to *All Men Are Enemies* to Hollywood almost ten years earlier;
in any event he had a lecture tour booked for January and
February. He disliked leaving Florida, but gas rationing,
Netta's lack of companionship there, and the closing of
the school were Catherine was to be sent forced his
decision. In September they left by car for California,
stopping off en route at Boulder to see friends made on
Aldington's earlier visit.

Aldington stayed in Hollywood for about three and a
half years. During that time he worked as a free-lance
writer for several motion picture companies with reasonable
financial success, but without ever finding the pot of gold
he probably hoped for. Obviously, his literary work
suffered to some extent, and yet he did produce a
surprising number of books during these years. He
finished *The Duke,* which was begun in Florida, and which
eventually won the James Tait Black Memorial Prize; he
wrote *The Romance of Casanova,* which was done on
commission for Columbia Pictures but was published as a
novel in New York and later in London; he edited *The
Portable Oscar Wilde,* using unpublished Wilde manuscripts
and letters from UCLA; and he translated *A Wreath for San
Gemignano* and *Great French Romances.* He also worked on an
Anthology of Verse in Translation (for the *Encyclopaedia
Britannica*), which was never published. When he left
Hollywood for Jamaica, where Netta's mother was building a
home, he was taking a rest on medical advice and hoped
after a few months to return. In an early letter from
Hollywood he says how much he likes the Los Angeles area
and that he will "never return to Europe"; just before

he left for Jamaica he said Hollywood had become a
madhouse and that he had been near to a nervous collapse
because of trying to do studio work and to write a book
at the same time.

Aldington drove from Hollywood to Mobile and then flew
to Jamaica where he arrived in May. By June he had given
up the idea of returning to Hollywood and thought of a
trip to Rio de Janeiro and Buenos Aires, "perhaps
returning to France in 1947," but in August 1946 he was
in New York en route to Paris, where he arrived in
September. The Aldingtons stayed in Paris until August of
1947, living first at a hotel on Boulevard Raspail and
then in a studio on the Boulevard Montparnasse. This was
a period of renewing old ties and arranging for the
publication of his work in various European countries
where wartime restrictions were ending. Aldington had
many of the problems that beset regular commerce: paper
shortages, blocked currencies, and various government
regulations, but between September of 1947 and February
of 1948 he earned nearly five thousand pounds in royalities.
By July the Aldingtons had to leave their studio; they flew
south to St. Clair, Le Lavandou, where they were to live
until the spring of 1951--Aldington felt as if he "had
come home after a long absence."

The relief from the commercial pressure of Hollywood
and the joy of being back on the Mediterranean coast of
France renewed Aldington's creative spirit. After he had
been there only a few months he wrote a friend that we was
halfway through an educational book he was doing for Evans
Brothers, nearly halfway through another anthology, and
had two more biographies and a novel in preparation. Some
of this work was, of course, started in Paris, but in the
four years following his return to France he published

Four English Portraits, The Strange Life of Charles Waterton, and his important biography, *D. H. Lawrence: Portrait of a Genius But.* . . . To the biographical works that he wrote during these highly productive years must be added his editions of *Walter Pater* and *The Religion of Beauty: Selections from the Aesthetes,* an introduction to a new edition of Jane Austen's work, and eleven introductions to the Penguin editions of Lawrence's books. Finally, his *Complete Poems* was published in 1948.

The year 1947 was important to Richard Aldington since it marked a renaissance in his creativity. It was also important in another respect: it was the year that Alister Kershaw, a young Australian poet who greatly admired Aldington's work, first met the man who was one of his literary heroes. Aldington helped the younger man to get established, and Kershaw repaid this kindness by becoming invaluable to him as his secretary and by literally providing a roof over Aldington's head in his last years. Reading a sampling of the twelve hundred letters Aldington wrote to Kershaw between 1947 and 1962, we can see how invaluably and unselfishly Kershaw served him. Another of the introductions that Aldington wrote during this period was to *A Bibliography of the Works of Richard Aldington from 1915 to 1948,* which Alister Kershaw prepared during these years at Le Lavandou.

In the spring of 1951 Aldington moved to Montpellier where he lived until 1957; his daughter Catherine was still with him, but sometime in 1950 his wife had decided to live permanently in England. Aldington visited Italy with his daughter in December of 1954 but, aside from short trips within France, these were years when the writer, who was now in his sixties, had lost some of the wanderlust of his youth. Besides, money was short and Aldington was fighting

for literary survival because of the two controversial
biographies, *Pinorman* and *Lawrence of Arabia*. There had
been criticism of the D. H. Lawrence biography when it
appeared in 1950; Aldington greatly admired Lawrence and
was one of his early champions, but in his biography he
reveals him as a human being as well as a great writer,
and some critics found that objectionable. *Pinorman*
aroused anger in British literary circles because of its
frank treatment of some of the foibles and weaknesses of
Aldington's friends Norman Douglas and Pino Orioli--
Douglas admirers in particular could not seem to
understand the biographer's dispassionate ability to
keep the man and his art in separate compartments.

But if publication of *Pinorman* brought a few critical
fieldpieces to bear in Aldington's directions, his *Lawrence
of Arabia* brought a barrage from critics, press, the
reading public, and what Aldington called the "Lawrence
Bureau." Beginning his T. E. Lawrence biography at the
suggestion of Alister Kershaw for whom Lawrence was a
boyhood hero, Aldington expected, as he says in his
introduction, that he would be writing the biography of
a hero, but as he progressed he realized that the TEL
legend was just that and mostly of Lawrence's own making.
Twenty years later most historians have come to accept
Aldington's version of the facts of Lawrence's life even
though the legend itself dies hard. In 1955, however,
even though Aldington prepared massive documentation, and
his publishers printed the book only because they knew he
could support his statements, the avalanche of abuse
heaped on Aldington was overwhelming and resulted in great
financial loss to the writer when publishers refused to
reprint his titles, bookstores refused to handle them, and
the hero-worshipping public refused to buy them. Only

legendary heroes such as St. George can safely slay a
dragon.

While Aldington devoted a large part of these years to
the extremely careful preparation of his T. E. Lawrence
biography (existing correspondence with friends who helped
him in his research verifies his caution), and to
defending it after publication, he still found time for
other literary work. Critical lectures he had given in
the United States on Pound and Eliot and on Housman and
Yeats were published in limited editions, and he wrote two
other biographies: one of the French poet Mistral, which
was awarded the 1959 Prix de Gratitude Mistralienne, and
the other of Robert Louis Stevenson. *Frauds* was inspired
by the stubborn gullibility of T. E. Lawrence's admirers;
there were also a number of introductions in French and
English to a series of books of photographs and some
additional D. H. Lawrence introductions.

Despite this continued literary activity and despite
the many previous titles which were in print at the
beginning of the decade, Aldington, after the release of
Lawrence of Arabia, found himself in serious financial
trouble. Even though this book was eminently successful
from a monetary angle, most of its royalties were being
funneled into a private trust intended to benefit
Aldington's daughter after his death. When his publishers
permitted his books to go out of print, claiming a hostile
press and reading public because of the T. E. Lawrence
biography, Aldington, who had supported himself by his pen
for over forty years, saw himself almost completely without
income. To add to his financial miseries he was behind
in his payments to the Patmores on the divorce settlement
made to them, and had to borrow 200 pounds from a friend
to avoid a writ and the bad publicity that would accompany

it. When Alister Kershaw came to Montpellier during the
Easter holidays of 1957 he saw the situation his friend
was in, and made plans to buy a small house in the Loire
Valley where Aldington and his daughter could live rent
free.

Aldington's last five years were happier than the
outlook early in 1957 promised, or than some of his
bitterest enemies may have hoped. In the first place his
literary fortune improved as the Lawrence affair died down.
A number of his works were brought back into print, if
not in England in other parts of the world, and
reprintings of the T. E. Lawrence biography itself were
called for. Although his doctor decided that his health
would permit no more books and he returned an advance on
a Balzac biography he had started, he was busy with other
literary work. He revised his D. H. Lawrence biography
for a German publisher, and translated, with Delano Ames,
the *Larousse Encyclopaedia of Mythology*. He wrote an
introduction for Volume III of Edward Nehls's *D. H.
Lawrence: A Composite Biography* to which he also
contributed in a recording session with others who had
also known Lawrence. There were three more books of
photographs for which he wrote introductions in English
and French, and an introduction to the fine D. H. Lawrence
critical biography by his good friend the French author
F.-J. Temple. The *Larousse*, and all the introductions to
the books of photography were arranged for him by an old
friend he had known since the early 1930s, Eric Warman.

Without doubt these last years were made comparatively
happy ones because of the loyalty of Richard Aldington's
friends. Alister Kershaw's part has been mentioned; in
1958 Aldington notes in a letter that a group of his
friends have contributed to a fund for him--he

particularly mentions the Duttons in Australia. And
during most of these last years there were substantial
gifts from Bryher, who first wrote to him about his poetry
when he was a soldier in the 1918 war, and who had been
a longtime friend to his first wife, H. D.

Because of the financial help he was getting, he was
able to travel more in these years than he had done during
the harrassed Montpellier years. For one thing, he spent
considerable time at Aix-en-Provence, close to his beloved
Mediterranean coast, to his daughter's school, and away
from the colder winters of the Berry. He visited Zürich
in 1959 in connection with Catherine's interest in
psychology and to see H. D. and Bryher, and Zagreb in the
summer of 1960, when he was probably visiting his
publishers there. In December of 1960 he was in Rome with
Catherine, and in the spring of 1961 he spent almost two
months in Venice--a final visit to the country that was so
important to him as a man and artist.

The very last journey that Aldington made must surely
have been one of his happiest. One of the bright spots in
all of the gloom of his literary fortunes following the
T. E. Lawrence biography was the constant and growing
demand for his work outside of England, particularly in
translation in Eastern Europe, and above all in Russia.
Although he grumbles in his correspondence about payments
that are not made or currency that is blocked, every so
often he is amazed by the size of a royalty payment that
comes through, especially from Russia where even he found
his popularity surprising. In 1957, because of his health,
he refused a suggestion from the Russian Writers' Union
that he celebrate his sixty-fifth birthday in Moscow. In
February of 1962, when the Writers' Union invited Catherine
and himself to spend three weeks in Russia as their guests,

Aldington agreed to celebrate his seventieth birthday there.

The Russians had been publishing Richard Aldington's work since *Death of a Hero*, and a large number of his novels and other books had been printed in the USSR, both in Russian and English. *All Men Are Enemies*, for example, was published in an edition of 225,000 copies and was quickly sold out. Indeed, Russian scholars were paying more attention to the British author than his own countrymen were. It was, therefore, a happy and fortunate thing that Aldington should be honored in this way just before his death. His accounts of his visit are heart warming to read.

There was sadness as well as happiness in these last years. One of the great sadnesses of old age is the loss of one's contemporaries, and Aldington in his letters reveals the grief he felt when dear friends such as Roy Campbell or Carl Fallas, whose death occurred only three months before his own, were lost to him. When H. D. died during the year before his own death, Aldington noted poignantly that her cremation had taken place on her wedding day. As the pages that follow show, his letters to H. D., which reach from their first separation by World War I to her death, are the second largest in number. The time between their trip to Paris in 1912 and the end of the Great War was "the good time," but perhaps a part of them remained always in love.

Richard Aldington returned home in mid-July and died on the 27th in the little house he usually referred to as "Chez Alister Kershaw." In 1974 I visited the hamlet of Maison Sallé which is located just over a vineyard-covered hill from Sury-en-Vaux. From the hill you can see in the distance the sharp rise on which is located the

fortress town of Sancerre that gives the wine of the
district its name. It is a peaceful, quiet place across
the Loire from where the main road goes through Cosne.
The farmers there remember Richard Aldington as a friend
and neighbor whom they loved, and whom they held in awe,
too (even though they may never have read any of his
work), in that curious way the French regard their artists.
Aldington's books still line the walls of almost every
room of the house in which he had lived, and somehow give
a feeling of his presence. They are also, in a way, an
oddity: all these books, many in English, tucked away
here in a French hamlet in the Loire valley. I visited
the small, walled graveyard where the wanderer from the
South Foreland is buried, and even that solidly English
"Richard Aldington" looked strangely lost on a simple
marble slab among the more elaborate stones engraved with
Gallic names.

II

Richard Aldington's literary works were produced over
the period of half a century and consist of some two
hundred titles which include poetry, essays and criticism,
translations, fiction, biography and autobiography,
editions and introductions. Such versatility and
productivity aroused criticism: Aldington himself said,
when his long poem *Life Quest* received adverse reviews,
that in the literary game the critics blew the whistle on
a successful novelist who wrote poetry. Furthermore, an
anonymous reviewer of the British edition of *Life For
Life's Sake* called Aldington a "journeyman of letters"
because of his long tenure and considerable production.
But many masters of letters have written prolifically over
a long period and in more than one genre. It is true,
however, that because of its extent and variety it is

difficult to evaluate Aldington's work fairly in a short
critical essay such as this. Fortunately, his writing in
the various genres is grouped roughly into time periods
when he was, for the most part, concerned with one literary
form, so that, at least, his work can be approached
chronologically.

Aldington says that when he was fifteen (1907) he
discovered Keats and began to write poetry. He was
hunting insects on the cliffs of the South Foreland "when
a line of iambic pentameter suddenly presented itself"; he
wrote it in his field notebook upside down in a symbolic
gesture. His *Complete Poems* was not published until 1948,
but it included no verse later than his long poem *The
Crystal World* which was first published in 1937. But even
these dates cover much more than the high time of
Aldington's poetry. Probably the decade 1910-20 could
fairly be said to be his poetic period; *Exile and Other
Poems* was published in 1923 but its poems were written
earlier, and the long poem *A Fool i' the Forest* (1924) is
a poetic preview of his novel *Death of a Hero*. After that
he wrote four more long poems: *The Eaten Heart* (1929) and
Love and the Luxembourg (1930) in a poetic renaissance
that celebrated the new course of his life in 1928; then
Life Quest (1935) and *The Crystal World*.

Between 1907 and 1910 Aldington produced a mass of
"poems" at least twice the size of his first collected
edition of 1928. He tried all of the formal verse types
from rhymed couplets to villanelles until he grew tired of
mimicry and began to write what he called "'rhythms', i.e.
unrhymed pieces with no formal metrical scheme where the
rhythm was created by a kind of inner chant." He says he
was influenced by the Greek choruses and Henley. Certainly
Aldington was familiar with the Greek classics before the

1912 Italian trip when he mentions reading Theocritus and
the *Greek Anthology;* most of the poems he sold to the
London newspapers which were published between February
and June in 1912 were translations--some from the Greek.
Besides, he surely read Greek as a schoolboy at Dover
College and later during his time at University College.
As for the influence of Henley, that too seems logical.
Professor de Solo Pinto in 1951 flatly called Henley's *In
Hospital* poems one of the points from which modern poetry
starts. At another time Aldington mentions Whitman as one
of his early interests--it would not be too difficult to
construct a crossing between modern free verse and the
Greek choruses using Henley and Whitman as closer stepping
stones.

Aldington must have been writing his "rhythms" in 1911
when he first showed Pound his work because Pound seeing
it said, "Well, I don't think you need any help from me."
In any event, the poems written by Aldington and H. D.
seemed to Pound to represent the trend of modern poetry
and the kind of poetry he was writing himself, so he
invented Imagism and launched H. D. and Aldington, in
Harriet Monroe's new *Poetry: A Magazine of Verse,* as
original Imagists. Aldington was worried about readers'
reaction to his vers libre and hoped it would not bring
undue criticism of Miss Monroe. "Choricos" and "To a
Greek Marble" are the two poems which appeared in that
issue of *Poetry* which launched Imagism as well as
Aldington's career; they are the first and second poems in
his *Complete Poems.*

Pound next consolidated the position of the Imagists by
editing their first anthology, *Des Imagistes,* in 1914; it
contained ten of Aldington's poems including two that had
first appeared in *Poetry.* Both the American and British

editions of *Des Imagistes* came under the critical fire of
reviewers who did not know quite what to say about this
strange new verse. Aldington was an even more important
influence on the next three Imagist anthologies, *Some
Imagist Poets*, published in 1915, 1916, and 1917, since he
not only contributed to them but also helped Amy Lowell
(she had seized the banner of Imagism from Pound who was
now doing battle for modern art under the flag of
Vorticism) to edit them. Reviews of these later
anthologies were better and there were even more of them;
Aldington wrote Amy Lowell, after the 1915 *Some Imagist
Poets*, that "opinion is beginning slightly to turn our
way."

When he was twenty-three, Aldington's first individual
volume of poetry was published by Harold Monro at his
Poetry Bookshop. *Images 1910-1915*, which appeared in
December 1915, contains thirty poems. An American edition
of this book with a slightly different content was
published by the Four Seas Company in 1916. These early
poems of Aldington's deal with the lost, ideal world which
is represented by Greece and the omnipresent, crass world
of contemporary London; in the best of them the poet heals
the breach between the real and the ideal. These are the
only poems not affected by Aldington's wartime experiences;
the poems immediately following these were written during
the war years, many while the poet was in France at the
front.

Two of Aldington's most attractive books of poetry were
published during 1917 by the private printer Reverend
Charles C. Bubb of Cleveland, Ohio. These dainty little
books were printed in very limited editions and only a
few survive. The first, *The Love Poems of Myrrhine and
Konallis*, was reprinted in 1926 by Pascal Covici in

Chicago in a much larger format with added poems and a
section of nineteen prose poems. The *Myrrhine and
Konallis* poems, which celebrate the lesbian love between
goat-girl and hetaira, are among the most beautiful of
Aldington's love poems; May Sinclair said they alone
should secure him a permanent place in literature. The
"Prose Poems" in the 1926 volume represent Aldington's
finest work in this form. The second of these booklets
that Bubb printed was *Reverie: A Little Book of Poems
for H. D.*, which Aldington considered representative of the
best of his trench work. Alec Waugh thought the title
piece "Reverie" a very lovely poem by one of the best
English war poets.

When Aldington returned to London early in 1919 he found
his poetry in demand and had no difficulty in arranging
for the publication of six books during the next two years.
C. W. Beaumont, who owned a small secondhand bookshop in
the Charing Cross Road, published a limited edition of
the war poems, *Images of War: A Book of Poems;* and Allen
and Unwin, a popular edition which was considerably
expanded. Also in 1919, Elkin Mathews published
Aldington's love poems, *Images of Desire,* and the Egoist,
Ltd., issued *Images* whose poems, for the most part, are
taken from his 1915 volume and the Imagist anthologies.
In the United States the Four Seas Company published the
love and war poems in one volume as *War and Love (1915-
1918)* and, two years later, an American edition of *Images
of War.* Obviously, 1919 was Aldington's *annus mirabilis:*
more than half of all his poetry was published during this
year. His firsthand encounter with the horror of war and
his sharp longing for the assuaging love of woman is
given artful form in these poems. The division between
his ideal world and the real one, only too starkly present,

was widened; the poet's increasingly difficult attempts
to bridge this gap provides part of the dramatic power
of these poems.

   The Berkshire Kennet, published separately in 1923, was
also included in Aldington's *Exile and Other Poems* of the
same year. The poems of the "Words for Music" section of
Exile, where "The Berkshire Kennet" appears, are highly
traditional and suggest the need the poet felt to steep
himself again in English poetry after so long a time away
from it. The poems of the "Exile" section, on the other
hand, reflect the poet's agony in trying to cast off the
effects of the war. While Aldington speaks of the second
part of this volume as "metrical exercises," it is
possible to see it as representative of the peace of soul
he was trying to reach during his Berkshire years, while
the "Exile" section portrays the actuality of his war-
wounded spirit.

   In 1925 the first of Aldington's five long poems, *A
Fool i' the Forest: A Phantasmagoria,* was published.
Because its subject is similar to that of Eliot's *The
Waste Land,* the miserable position into which
contemporary humanity has gotten itself, the suggestions
of influence were inevitable. *A Fool,* however, is a much
different poem, and has been called by some critics
Aldington's best. It is a far more personal poem, whose
three speaking characters represent aspects of modern man.
Like them, Aldington spent a considerable period of his
life "visiting" Greece, and thought that some part of him
had been "murdered" in France. A second long poem *The Eaten
Heart,* was published in a limited edition in 1928 by Nancy
Cunard's Hours Press, and, some years later, with other
poems in a popular edition. Based on "the old Provence
tale of the Eaten Heart," Aldington attempts to deal with

the essential loneliness of human existence by suggesting
the love of another as the only escape.

In 1928 the first collection of Aldington's poetry was
published in New York; a British edition followed in
1929. A less expensive *Collected Poems* was published in
England in 1933 and another American collection in 1934.
The final collection, *The Complete Poems of Richard
Aldington*, was published in London by Allan Wingate in
1948. Just as the year 1919 marked the publication of
many of Aldington's books of poetry, a decade later would
show similar activity. Besides the collected poems in
England and the United States, and the limited edition
of *The Eaten Heart*, Aldington published during the next
year another long poem called *Love and the Luxembourg* in
the American edition and *A Dream in the Luxembourg* in the
British edition. The poem is a paean to that love between
man and woman which, in *The Eaten Heart*, the poet suggests
is the only answer to human solitude; it has a sensuous
Keatsian quality reminiscent of *The Love of Myrrhine and
Konallis*. Also in this year Aldington edited *Imagist
Anthology 1930: New Poetry by the Imagists* to show that
the original Imagists were by no means dead as poets. "The
Eaten Heart" and two other poems appeared as Aldington's
contribution.

Richard Aldington's rarest book of poetry is *Movietones.
Invented and Set Down by Richard Aldington, 1928-1929*.
Only ten copies were privately printed in 1932; all of
the poems are new except "Hark the Herald," which was
printed by the Hours Press in 1928 as a satiric Christmas
card. Like the *Myrrhine and Konallis* poems, none of
these is reprinted in Aldington's final collection of his
poetry. Many of the *Movietones* poems are wry comments on
the shortcomings of contemporary life. Aldington wrote

his long poem *Life Quest* in 1934 while convalescing from
an automobile injury. It is an important poem to an
understanding of the poet since it so clearly expresses
his idea of "life for life's sake"--it repeats the message
of all of his postwar poetry: love while there is time.
The Crystal World, published two years later in 1937, is
the last of the five long poems and Aldington's last
individual volume of poetry before *The Complete Poems.*
It is fittingly a love poem--it celebrates his love for
Netta, his second wife, but is is also a poem about poetry.

The total body of Richard Aldington's poetry is
considerable--in quantity more than Eliot's and less than
Lawrence's. Between these two poets Aldington much
preferred the work of Lawrence, although, as the letters
show, both were his early friends. Aldington believed
Lawrence and not Eliot followed the authentic poetic line.
Certainly much of the emotion in Aldington's work which
he felt essential to good poetry is Lawrentian. Emotion,
passion, sensuousness, life--these were the keystones of
Richard Aldington's poetic art. His dominant form, the
long cadenced line, he felt depended primarily on its
ability to express individual emotion; the whole body of
his poetry celebrates the life of the here and now. It
may be that his war experience widened the chasm between
the real and ideal realms of his youthful poetry, and
that all of his postwar poems are a magnificent human
effort to heal over that breach as the body heals its
wounds with the warm blood of life itself.

Although Aldington published poetry in the 1920s (and
other works which are considered below), his principal
efforts at this time were in the field of literary
criticism and journalism. Even as early as 1912 he
mentions an article in a daily and another in a weekly and

that he was doing reviews for Monro's *Poetry Review*. The
next year he became literary editor of *The New Freewoman,*
which was eventually renamed *The Egoist.* Here he was the
champion of Imagism and of contemporary poetry in general;
in addition, his essays on and reviews of current French
writers did much to influence his associates and the
trend of modern poetry. He continued this early
journalism, which included writing for periodicals other
than *The Egoist,* until his war duty intervened, at which
time Eliot took over his *Eogist* post. None of this early
work was collected, but it is discussed and some of it
reprinted in Cyrina N. Pondrum's *The Road from Paris*
(1974). Professor Pondrum sees Aldington as one of the
early critics who renewed English interest in French
literature, and thereby influenced modern poetry.

When Aldington returned from the war he was able to make
or renew important connections with a number of literary
journals. Most important was his assignment with the
Times Literary Supplement to review French books, and
his position as assistant editor on Eliot's *Criterion.*
Literary Studies and Reviews, published in 1924, reprints
articles from both the *Times* and *Criterion* and also the
Monthly Chapbook, the *New Statesman* and the *English Review*
in England and the *Literary Review* and the *Dial* in the
United States. *French Studies and Reviews,* published
in 1926, collects from the *Times Literary Supplement* and
the *Criterion.*

Commenting on these two collections of essays in his
study of Aldington's literary career, Selwyn Kittredge says
their main interest is French literature and its influence
on English writers. French critic and writer F.-J. Temple
notes that Aldington was the first in England to recognize
the genius of Marcel Proust. Not all of the essays from

these two collections have to do with French literature:
in "The Poetry of T. S. Eliot," an essay written before
the publication of *The Waste Land*, Aldington commends Eliot
as a poet "who had brought new vigour to the intellectual
tradition of English poetry," even though Aldington did
not himself feel that Eliot's poetry led in a direction he
wished to go. He is also remarkably perceptive in his
essay "Mr. James Joyce's 'Ulysses'" written before *Ulysses*
was published in book form and before *Finnegans Wake*, of
course. He saw *Ulysses* as a remarkable accomplishment
which he was convinced would have a deplorable effect on
young writers who tried to imitate it. One of the marks
of a fine critic is this ability to recognize genius
whether or not its particular manifestation is to his
taste.

In 1935 Aldington's *Artifex: Sketches and Ideas* was
published. It is a curious mixture of the familiar essay,
the "character," and what its author calls "literary
echoes." The book takes its title from an essay on the
caves of Altamira where Artifex is identified as "servant
of the life impulse, maker of myths, music and images."
There is also an essay on Charles Waterton about whom
Aldington was later to write a biography. In style
Artifex prefigures Aldington's autobiography which he
was to write five years later. Alister Kershaw in 1970
edited another collection of Aldington's essays, *Richard
Aldington: Selected Critical Writings, 1928-1960*. This
fourth book brings together work which originally appeared
in periodicals, as pamphlets, and as Aldington's
introductions to authors he edited, or to the books of
others. As Kershaw says in his introduction, this is a
very small selection from Aldington's considerable body
of critical writing. Professor Harry T. Moore, who

contributes a preface to this collection, sees the essay
on Remy de Gourmont as a valuable introduction to this
writer; Moore also says he does not know of a better
critical essay on Pater than the one Kershaw includes.

These collections, together with the much larger body
of his uncollected critical work, show Richard Aldington
holding firmly to his ideas of the proper stance for the
critic which was not, as Alister Kershaw puts it, to use
the work of others as a platform for his own "act," but
to direct attention to what he considers good work, to
suggest why he thinks it good, and then to step out of
the way and let the reader see for himself. Indeed, this
same sensibility and sensitivity that informs all of
Richard Aldington's work is particularly valuable to
his criticism.

The publication, in 1929, of Richard Aldington's first
novel, *Death of a Hero*, catapulted him from the relative
obscurity of a poet and man of letters onto the public
stage as a popular novelist. Ten years after the Great
War, Aldington needed to try again to write it out of his
unconscious as he had previously tried to do in his war
poems. As a matter of fact, many of the exact images
that were used in the war poems reappear in this first
novel. *Death of a Hero* was one of a wave of war novels
that appeared at about the same time; almost as though
the necessary period of artistic incubation had passed
and fiction writers were now able to deal with the war
experience. It could have been, too, that the reading
public needed a sufficient passage of time before they
were able to confront the war experience with some
objectivity.

In any event, its hour arrived: *Death of a Hero*, a
smashing popular and critical success, launched Aldington

on a new phase of his writing career which would see him
publish eight novels and two collections of short stories,
all, except one of them, in the ten-year period between
1929 and 1939. While he also published poetry, a volume
of essays, several anthologies, and even a play (with
Derek Patmore) during this same period, it can be seen as
a time when Aldington was devoting himself primarily to
fiction, just as during the previous decade he had done
mostly critical journalism and translation and the decade
before that, poetry.

Contemporary reviewers and later critics of *Death of a
Hero*, as Professor Kittredge points out, for the most part
saw the novel as a powerful and realistic depiction of the
war. George Orwell, for instance, called it "the best
of the English war books, at least of those describable
as novels." What Aldington was really interested in,
however, was the effects of the war on those who survived
it and, even more importantly, in the weakness of the
social structure that made war possible in the first place.
Sidney Rosenthal, in his study of Aldington's fiction,
suggests that the novel was not simply a protest against
war, but a study in self-deception which offers a number
of satirical portraits to show how individual deception
leads to national deception. To Aldington, the war
itself, once underway, seems to have an understandable
though bitter logic in which its participants play
heroically the roles allotted them. Aldington saves his
sharpest satire for the "Victorianism" that led to the
war, and his greatest pity for those who were destroyed
by it whether or not they physically survived it.

Aldington himself spoke of *Roads to Glory* (1930) as
being "a kind of hangover from *Death of a Hero*." Critical
response to this first collection of short stories was

unfavorable; mostly, it seems, because of an inability
to accept Aldington's keen satire as implying the kind of
concern about humanity that always attaches to true satire.
Professor Rosenthal sees the stories as depictions of
individual characters who represent the life-stifling
ideologies Aldington opposed. The other collection of
short stories, *Soft Answers* (1932), is quite different
from the first group. Harry Moore, in his preface to
the 1967 "Crosscurrents" edition, speaks of them as
"slightly satiric, the kind of personal satires that
might be called caricatures." Rosenthal feels these
stories are as close to Swiftian satire as Aldington was
to come. Most of the targets of Aldington's lampoons
can be easily identified, so that one has the choice of
considering them personal satire, as Moore does, or
more broadly, as satires of human attitudes, which is
the way Rosenthal sees them. Kittredge makes an important
comment when he notes Aldington's ability to recognize
the great artistry of men like Pound and Eliot while still
being able to puncture their human foibles--a trait
Aldington carries forward to his biographical writing of
the next decade.

In *The Colonel's Daughter* (1931), the novel which follows
Death of a Hero, Aldington switches his satiric attack
entirely to the home front, taking aim at the middle-class
English villager. The author himself felt that this novel
was rather closely connected with his first one because its
heroine was crippled not only by the smothering society
around her, but also because the war had destroyed so
many of her possible husbands. With *All Men Are Enemies*
(1933) Aldington begins what Rosenthal considers a series
of romantic novels which, while they still focus on the
destructive results of conventional and formalized

approaches to human life, lack the bite and satirical
power of the two earlier novels and some of the short
stories. In *Seven Against Reeves* (1938) and *Casanova*,
the novel written in Hollywood and published in 1946,
Rosenthal sees Aldington recovering his comic view and,
in the actions of his two heroes, pointing out the
foolishness of any sort of formula for the enjoyment of
life.

Kittredge believes *Women Must Work* (1934) a better novel
than its predecessor even though the plot is similar with
the exception that its hero is a woman. This time, still
concerned with the destructive effects of the war,
Aldington changes his attack to the wealthy upper-middle
classes blaming them for ignoring the conditions that led
to the war and for permitting their children to be
educated to accept war as a glorious enterprise. Again
Aldington's main theme is that the individual cannot
survive within England's rigid class structure and must
either be smothered or escape in exile. *Very Heaven* (1937)
continues the task that Aldington had set for himself: to
give through his novels a picture of his times with World
War I as a focal point. Both Kittredge and Rosenthal,
however, think this was the least successful of the novels,
wavering as it does between satire and romance and lacking
the narrative control of the earlier works.

Rejected Guest (1939) was the last of the novels written
during the 1930s and the last of Aldington's novels except
for the postwar *Casanova* (1946). Contemporary reviews
were good; Mary Colum notes that the first hundred pages
in particular make excellent reading. Selwyn Kittredge
accounts for this by pointing out that this first section
is almost pure narrative and is written with the same
economy and sureness that characterizes the last part of

Death of a Hero. Rosenthal sees a revival of Aldington's
ability to maintain a tension between sentiment and irony
which is defined by the distance he is able to maintain
between his own viewpoint and that of his protagonist who,
in the first part of the novel, speaks convincingly in
his fictional voice.

The fiction of Richard Aldington is characterized by
the same kind of split that is evident in his poetry,
although it cannot be described in exactly the same terms.
In the poetry the opposites are the real and the ideal and
Aldington often used classical Greece as a metaphor for
his perfect time and place the same as Yeats used
Byzantium. In his early poetry, Aldington's "real" is
often the commonplace environment of contemporary times:
the moviehouse of "Cinema Exit," the subway train of "In
the Tube," or the dirty seaport town in "Childhood"--the
ultimate "real" is the holocust of 1914-18 which the poet
faced in *Images of War*. On some level, Aldington was
aware of these opposites within himself which caused him
to see the world with a split vision, because, while he
wrote some fine poems set in his ideal world and some
true ones in settings of harsh reality, his most successful
poems--I think of "Interlude"--are able with great effort
of artistic concentration and control, to link both worlds
in the timelessness of art or of love.

By the time of the novels, however, a subtle change has
taken place. In his "Author's Note" to *All Men Are
Enemies,* Aldington writes of his hero as "an example of
the modern romantic idealistic temperment." The ideal
perfection once symbolized by the unattainable classical
Greece has been merged with the more romantic and more
possible escape in this time and place--in the novel,
the island of Aeaea and Katha's arms. Possibly this is

the compromise one makes at thirty-eight in adjusting from
one's views at eighteen. If so, the compromise that
Aldington has made, by the time of the novels, with his
pole of reality is an even more interesting one. In the
poems the real must be disarmed by the artistic effort of
binding it to the ideal as Aldington did, for instance, in
"Bombardment" where the soldiers ". . . looked above the
wreckage of the earth/To where the white clouds moved in
silent lines/Across the untroubled blue." In the novels,
Aldington is still dissatisfied with the reality of much
of the world around him, but now his strategy has changed:
he views it satirically and cuts that he may cure.

If the long poem *A Fool i' the Forest* foreshadows
Death of a Hero, surely *Love in the Luxembourg* prefigured
All Men Are Enemies. Both have elements of satire and
romance, but certainly the first pair leans to the
satiric view of reality and the second to the romantic
possibilities of an escape, if only a temporary one, from
reality to an ideal place of love. Critics usually see
this duality in all of Aldington's novels and most, like
Kittredge and Rosenthal, see the more openly satiric novels
as Aldington's best vein. Sir William Haley, on the
other hand, picks *Death of a Hero* and *All Men Are Enemies*
as the two novels that will stand. Indeed, is not
Aldington's position the very human one of vacillating
between remaking the world outside of the gates or
trying frantically to get back into the garden?

Although Aldington's achievement in the field of
biography belongs to the 1940s and 1950s, his first and
one of his finest biographies, *Voltaire,* was published in
New York and London as early as 1925. In the midst of the
great storm of controversy which swirled around the later
biographies, no one seemed to remember Aldington's fine

Voltaire which, even this early in his career, indicated
his natural bent toward biography. The *Dial* review said
of *Voltaire*'s author, "He has, indeed, a most rare
equipment, the critical sense, combined with the
historical perspective, personal intensity, and literary
craft." The *New Statesman*'s reviewer saw correctly that
"it would remain the standard English short biography for
many years" as it has. Aldington did not attempt any
full-scale work in this medium until after he reached the
United States in 1939, although he produced shorter works
on D. H. Lawrence, Remy de Gourmont, Maugham, and Charles
Waterton.

In the fall of 1939 Aldington realized that if he ever
did return to Europe it would not be to the one he had
left, and he proposed to his American publisher, Viking
Press, a book which he originally wanted to call "Adieu
Europa." He planned, he said, to treat himself "as a
psychological problem, a study of the interaction of a
temperament and an environment"--the result was his
autobiography, *Life For Life's Sake,* published as a book
in 1941 after being serialized in the *Atlantic Monthly*.
The style and tone of this work recall *Artifex:* it is
frank and open in respect to his interactions with people
and places, but does not delve into his intimate private
life. As a book about an extremely interesting
personality it holds the reader's close attention; as a
work which reminisces about the people and happenings
of the decades of 1910-40 it is a fascinating and
valuable study.

Aldington's next book, *The Duke*, was one of several
projects he suggested to his publisher and may have been
selected by them because the time was appropriate in
those dark days of World War II to recall England's

former glory. There were other good Wellington
biographies, especially Guedalla's, so that Aldington
needed a unique approach. He found this first by
adopting the easy style of his autobiography (for
instance, in his opening chapter he accounts for his
initial interest in Wellington by narrating incidents
from his boyhood near Walmar Castle which was the Duke's
home); and secondly, by pitching the tone of his work to
a general cultivated reading audience rather than a
scholarly one. Aldington also made sure that he mustered
the necessary scholarly material, but, except for a
wittily annotated bibliography, avoids the documentation
that so often stands in the way of reading pleasure. When
it appeared in 1943 *The Duke* won high praise from most
reviewers and was eventually given the James Tait Black
Memorial Award for biography.

Aldington calls his *Four English Portraits, 1801-1851*
(1948) "sketches" which were "designed as an introduction
or supplement to more serious studies of nineteenth-
century history and biography." He chose four characters
to touch four different strata of society in the first
half of the century; one of these was the eccentric Charles
Waterton about whom an essay, originally written in 1932
as a leader in the *Times Literary Supplement* and reprinted
by Heinemann for private circulation, appears in *Artifex*.
Aldington must have found Waterton interesting because,
with the encouragement of Evans Brothers, who published
Four English Portraits, he made him the subject of his
next biography, *The Strange Life of Charles Waterton,*
in 1949. Neither of these books (in one of his letters
he calls them "textbooks") was as significant as *The
Duke* or the biography published next, *D. H. Lawrence:
Portrait of a Genius But.* . . (1950).

It is important to recall that D. H. Lawrence was a
major influence on Aldington's life and work, and, further,
that Aldington had been actively defending and critically
praising Lawrence's work in a series of articles,
introductions, essays, and monographs dating from the
1920s and before--indeed, he once called him "the most
interesting human being I have known." Lawrence had an
irresistable appeal to one side of Aldington (Aldington's
introduction to *Apocalypse* [1932] reveals this), but
Aldington's cooler, more dispassionate side, the source
of his powers as a satirist, added the "But" to the title
he gave his friend's biography. Most of the numerous
memoirs and reminiscences written between Lawrence's
death and Aldington's book had been one-sided views;
Aldington tried to show the whole man and wrote the first
good biography of Lawrence. Aldington thought it possible
for genius to have human failings, and he delineated
Lawrence's as fearlessly as he did those aspects of
Lawrence he admired without reservation. Unfortunately,
this satisifed neither those critics who wished to
disparage Lawrence nor those who wished to revere him;
nonetheless, although it has been superseded in general
by the work of men such as Harry T. Moore, it remains a
vital book for anyone interested in D. H. Lawrence.

*Pinorman. Personal Recollections of Norman Douglas, Pino
Orioli, and Charles Prentice* (1954) only further eroded
Aldington's reputation as a biographer with those critics
and readers who preferred not to see some truths in print.
Written in an informal, even colloquial style, *Pinorman*
is composed of a ragbag collection of memories filled out
with old letters and notes, all of which Aldington intended
should be useful to future biographers. When Aldington
frankly discussed Douglas's homosexuality he aroused a

hornets' nest of the older author's friends in the literary
world who reacted at once and fiercely. Oddly enough,
anyone reading Aldington's letters over the span of years
he knew these old friends, will be convinced that he felt
only kindness toward them despite any individual foibles,
but, once again, "the logic of facts is irresistible" to
Aldington and he withholds nothing.

The angry buzzings that greeted *Pinorman* were nothing
to the roar of outrage that arose when Collins published
Lawrence of Arabia. A Biographical Enquiry in 1955.
Aldington says in his "Introductory Letter to Alister
Kershaw" (and this has been confirmed to me by Kershaw)
that he began this biography "with the hope of
investigating a hero and his deeds"; what he did was
destroy a romantic legend that had been created and
nurtured by Lawrence himself and embraced unquestioningly
by both Britain and America. Again Aldington revealed
the facts as he found them, and despite the howls of
Lawrence's friends, the British literary establishment
and sundry others, these facts have never been disproved
but have been added to over the last twenty years to the
extent that the legendary Lawrence of Arabia must now be
seen for what he is: a literary artist of considerable
skill who, in his personal life, was a consummate fake.
The interesting question is, aside from his dispassionate
love of truth, why did Aldington bother to pursue a line
of inquiry and publish findings that he must have known
would severely affect his then secure position in the
literary world? Professor Kittredge suggests that
Aldington so hated fakery of all kinds that he could not
stop himself from revealing this super-fraud who became
the scapegoat for all of the falsity and deception
Aldington saw in the world around him.

In his later years, Aldington wrote another book of
portraits, *Frauds* (1957), which, as noted, was a response
to the gullibility of T. E. Lawrence followers, and two
more biographies. *Introduction to Mistral* (London 1956
and Carbondale, Illinois, 1960) won Aldington the rare
honor (for a non-French writer) of being awarded the Prix
de Gratitude Mistralienne for 1959. Harry Moore, in his
Preface to the 1960 edition, quotes Cyril Upton, Riviera
correspondent of the *Times* (London) as saying, "I have
read many studies of Mistral, but this Introduction is, in
my opinion, by far the most intelligent approach that has
been accomplished." The last biography, *Portrait of a
Rebel. The Life and Work of Robert Louis Stevenson* was in
the series of texts produced by Evans Brothers, Ltd., and
was recently published in Moscow in translation.

Richard Aldington's approach to biography was somewhat
unusual. He shied away from calling his books
"biographies," and usually substituted a term such as
"portrait," "recollection," or "enquiry." He may have
done this because he was unsure of his credentials and
felt that the documented biography belonged to the
academician; it seems more likely, however, from the tone
of the best of these works, that he was not trying to
catch the ear of a scholarly audience or of a popular one
but was trying to reach a cultured, well-read audience
(which, incidently, may no longer have existed), who
would turn aside from the formalities of a scholarly
biography. What happened, however, was that his lucid
style, warm tone, passion for truth, and hatred of humbug
of any kind, coupled with his eventual commitment to a
position vis-à-vis his subjects, brought him a wider
albeit more diverse audience than he had hoped for--a
living audience, too, since many of his biographies are

currently in print.

The last two categories of Aldington's works do not fit into convenient time slots, but extend over all of his productive years. In his autobiography, Aldington tells how, under the urging of his mentor, Dudley Grey, he taught himself French and started on Italian. As an English schoolboy in the early part of this century, he must already have been introduced to Latin and Greek, and some of the early poems he sold to the *Evening Standard* and *Pall Mall Gazette* early in 1912 were translations. One of Aldington's accomplishments as literary editor of the *Egoist* was the Poets' Translation Series, which was to make the classic poets available to the modern reader in translation by contemporary poets. He himself accounted for five of the series which started in 1915; four of these were collected in 1940 as *Medallions*. His first prose translation, in 1916 and with John Cournos, was Sogolub's *The Little Demon*. Since Aldington did not know Russian, his task probably was to rewrite Cournos's literal rendering.

Most of Aldington's translations date from the 1920s, his decade devoted to reviewing and criticism when he was writing on French books for the *Times Literary Supplement*. During these years he was reading continuously in French and Italian and had taught himself to read Old French. His first translation, Goldoni's *The Good-Humoured Ladies,* was done in 1922 as a commission from C. W. Beaumont, who had printed the limited edition of *Images of War* three years before. Then an article on Cyrano's *Voyages Imaginaires* for the *Supplement* occasioned an inquiry from the publishers, Routledge, which brought a commission to translate Cyrano's book. This fortunate connection resulted in a series of ten translations which

Aldington did for this publisher in a five-year period.
He also edited for Routledge a series of other translations
from eighteenth-century French authors and made a
translation of a modern French book, Julien Benda's *La
Trahison des Clercs* (published as *The Great Betrayal* in
London and *The Treason of the Intellectuals* in New York).

During these same years Aldington's translation of *The
Mystery of the Nativity* (1924) was published under the
imprint of the Medici Society, and his translation of
Pierre Custot's "curious" book about oceanography, *Sturly*
(1924), was published by Jonathan Cape. This last
translation brought about an early connection between
T. E. Lawrence and Aldington, who was asked to translate
it when Lawrence was unable to cope with the technical
words used: Aldington says he solved the problem by
comparing English and French scientific textbooks and
using the common denominator of the Latin word to find
the right English translation for the French word. Custot
was so impressed that he invited Aldington to the aquarium
at Monte Carlo, believing him a fellow scientist.

One of the literary projects that Aldington had hoped
would continue his Poets' Translation Series in a new
direction was a collection of Romance lyric texts with
translations and comments. Crosby Gaige came to see him
in Berkshire in the late 1920s and agreed to publish such
an anthology to be printed by the famous bookman, Bruce
Rogers; the 1928 limited edition of *Fifty Romance Lyric
Poems* was followed by a popular one in London in 1931. In
1945, when he was living in Hollywood, Aldington heard
about the destruction of the town of San Gemignano; in its
memory he wrote an essay and translated Folgore de San
Gemignano's "The Garland of Months," both of which were
published as *A Wreath for San Gemignano*. This charming

little book is illustrated by Aldington's second wife
Netta, and in its introductory essay Aldington quotes from
his note on Folgore in *Fifty Romance Lyric Poems*. This was
his last book of poetry in translation.

Remy de Gourmont had been a favorite author since *Egoist*
days when Richard Aldington had reviewed de Gourmont's
work enthusiastically, and even helped him financially
by soliciting money for him from Amy Lowell. Aldington's
essay on de Gourmont was published in 1928 and in the
same year Aldington translated *Selections from All His
Works* which was followed in 1931 by a translation of de
Gourmont's *Letters to the Amazon*. Critics of the Modern
period agree that de Gourmont was an important influence
so that Aldington's writings on him and translations of
his work were significant.

Chatto and Windus planned to have Aldington do
translations of all the classical Greek drama, but the
depression intervened and only the *Alcestis* (1930) was
published; however, in 1932, this same publisher brought
out a limited edition of Gérard de Nerval's *Aurelia*
translated by Aldington. In his introduction to this work,
Aldington reviews his translations from the French: the
purpose of the translations published during the years
1923-29, he says, was the possibly quixotic one of
revealing to the "'general public' (for what is unknown
to scholars?) certain neglected authors between the
fifteenth and nineteenth centuries" who he "'discovered'
while adventuring among French books." Aldington also bids
a "temporary farewell" to his translating in England
saying that until 1932 at least he expects to be occupied
with other work for the United States. The introduction is
dated 1929 from Fabrégas, Var, so it is evident that he was
working on his translations for Gaige, but he was probably

also finishing his *Decameron* for Covici, Friede who
published it in 1930. A friend recently gave me a Dell
Laurel Edition of Aldington's translation of *The Decameron*
which was very much alive in its sixth printing during
the period 1962-69.

Following *Aurelia* (1932) there are no translations until
A Wreath for San Gemignano in 1945. In that year Aldington
also wrote his friend Eric Warman about a new publisher
called Pilot Press who had asked him to supply an
introduction to some translated French novels. The book,
Great French Romances, published in 1946, has a thirty-four
page introduction by Aldington who also selected the four
novels which include *Dangerous Acquaintances,* by Chonderlos
de Laclos, translated by Aldington in 1925 as a part of the
Routledge series. In 1958 the same Eric Warman was
instrumental in getting Aldington his last translating
work: the *Larousse Encyclopaedia of Mythology* which he
translated with Delano Ames. Aldington's many letters to
Warman (listed in the pages following) show how meticulous
he was with his translating work, and how anxious to find
the precise word to convey in English the author's exact
meaning.

"To convey the author's exact meaning"--this is
certainly the first task of the translator, and his success
can be measured accurately only by the critic whose
understanding is sensitive to the subtleties of both
languages. Even without this gauge, however, distinctions
can be made. For instance, the idiom Aldington uses in
his prose translations is the same lucid, pleasing, and
economical style that marks his own works; his
translations of poetry convey the emotion that is so
important to his own poetry while still preserving the
uniqueness of the original so that translated poems of

Anyte of Tegea, for instance, are not at all like those
of Meleager of Gadara. A more prosaic measure of the
success of Aldington's translations is the simple fact
that so many of them are still in print and are often the
definitive translation: in 1973 the Limited Editions Club
of New York selected Aldington's translation for its
Candide; among its 1974 Special Publications, the Folio
Society of London lists *The Decameron* in "Richard
Aldington's unexpurgated translation." From the time of
the Poets' Translation Series in 1915 Aldington wanted
passionately to bring literature from other languages
and other ages to his readers, and his labor of translation
was a labor to share with others the discoveries he had
made while adventuring among books.

An important feature of many of Richard Aldington's
translations was the biographical and critical
introductions which he supplied. In the translations he
did for Routledge and in the Broadway Library series he
both translated and edited, his carefully written essays
are still among the best critical-biographical
introductions in English to these authors.

Aldington, of course, wrote many introductions to books
he did not translate or edit. Early in his own fiction-
writing career he introduced two works by James Hanley,
and late in his life he wrote introductions in French
and English for a series of books of photographs of
Italy, Austria, France, and Switzerland, drawing on his
own intimate knowledge of these countries. By far the
greatest number of introductions he wrote for work not his
own were those he prepared for the books of his friend
D. H. Lawrence, beginning shortly after Lawrence's death
in 1930.

These introductions carry on the unflagging critical

support Aldington gave Lawrence from the days of the
Imagist anthologies and *The Egoist*. They begin with the
essay introducing *Apocalypse* (1932), which is in the form
of a letter to Frieda Lawrence, and extend through the
long series of Penguin Lawrences of the 1950s. These are
all extremely valuable and most are still in print; they
were written by a critic who revered Lawrence (he closed
his letter-to-Frieda Introduction of *Apocalypse* ". . .
and all my reverence for the great English writer who was
your husband"), and who also knew him--in the introduction
to *Selected Essays* Aldington gives credit to "personal
knowledge of his life." Most of these Lawrence
introductions give biographical and bibliographic
information; they are all valuable to any Lawrence student
and to the general reader; and they are readable--
Aldington is sometimes wrongheaded, but never dull.

Aldington and Guiseppe Orioli also very ably edited
Lawrence's *Last Poems* (1932), and Aldington anthologized
a selection of Lawrence's magnificent descriptive prose
in *The Spirit of Place* (1935), and compiled a selection of
his letters and essays for the Penguin series. His
interest in Lawrence lasted throughout his life: in his
late sixties, only a few years before his death, he
introduced volume III of Edward Nehls's *D. H. Lawrence:
A Composite Biography* and the study of the French
critic F.-J. Temple, *D. H. Lawrence: l'oeuvre et la vie*.

Besides his collaboration with Orioli, and his editorship
of the Broadway Translation series, Richard Aldington was
a fine book editor in other fields. *Oscar Wilde* (1946),
Walter Pater (1948), and *The Religion of Beauty* (1950),
taken with their impressive introductions, may well provide
the best available survey of the literature of the
aesthetes of the late nineteenth century. One of

Aldington's great works of editing was *The Viking Book of Poetry of the English Speaking World* first published in 1941, revised and published as a two-volume edition in 1958 and a one-volume edition in 1962, the year of his death. Once the anthology was decided on, Aldington took almost two years to make his selections and write the introduction. As an epigraph he quotes some lines from Pope beginning "'Tis with our judgments as our watches, none/Go just alike, yet each believes his own," which nicely defines the anthologist's problem. Aldington was disappointed by some adverse criticism, but generally critical acceptance was warm. Mark Van Doren called Aldington's anthology, "The best comprehensive anthology of British and American poetry yet made," and Allen Tate predicted that "It ought with ease to succeed in replacing the other comprehensive anthologies in the field"--the 1941 edition sold almost one hundred thousand copies. Aldington tried, as he tells us in his introduction, to keep the poems and poets that one expects to find in an anthology, but to use his personal taste to collect less obvious poems around this nucleus. A measure of his success is the inclusion of thirteen selections from Melville, a poet whose work had been sadly neglected by all previous anthologists; indeed, Aldington wrote Pascal Covici in 1940 expressing surprise that the only complete edition of Melville's poems was British and urged that Viking prepare "a complete and properly edited Herman Melville, who is probably the greatest writer America has yet produced."

Elsewhere, writing of Richard Aldington as a poet, I argue that although he may not be as important as some of his contemporaries, he is more representative of his times.

Having a body of his poetry from before, during, and after
World War I makes it possible to trace the effects of
this most important single event of the first third of the
century on a sensitive artist of that time. Looking at
all of Aldington's work for the half-century between 1912
and 1962 suggests that a similar case can be made for
him as one of the most representative *writers* of this
period. He produced good work in many genres over a long
stretch of time, so that not only the changes the passing
decades bring in it can be seen, but it also presents a
variety of perspectives from which to view his responses.
What emerges is a pattern which indicates that his
artistic answer to the human situation represents what
most sensitive men of his time were feeling.

Writing of D. H. Lawrence, Aldington said he "was a very
complex and self-contradictory person, in whom two hostile
selves seemed always struggling for mastery." This is
probably true of Lawrence, and it is certainly true of
Aldington. As a matter of fact, when Lawrence read
Aldington's first critical essay he said it was more
about Richard than about himself. Obviously there was much
in Lawrence's makeup that attracted Aldington to him;
one of these attractions may have been the divided
personalities they shared. Aldington's poetry tries to
bridge a split between his real and ideal worlds; the
novels reflect a similar double view in his satiric
effort to cure the world and his romantic effort to
escape it. Richard Aldington seems to have had these
forces of Romanticism and Classicism warring within
himself all of his life; his work reveals opposing
Appollonian-Dionysian drives and is thus representative
of the plight of twentieth-century man who seems torn
between ordering his universe and trying to escape it.

One of the curiosities of Aldington's life is the fact
that he never visited Greece although he traveled to
Italy many times. It may have been that he was
unconsciously protecting the ideal place from desecration
by reality--that he was not able finally to heal the split
between them. To arrive at such firm conclusions about
Richard Aldington's work and life is, however, an
unfinished task--certainly it has been a neglected one
even though he has now been dead for almost fifteen years.
We may hope this Checklist of his magnificent letters
will encourage others to begin this assessment.

2

Repository Symbols

Unless listed below, private holders are identified individually or by "recipient" if letters are held by the addressee. Letters unavailable for general study are marked *"restricted."*

BM = British Museum Library, London.

BU = Boston University, University Libraries, Boston.

C = Jonathan Cape, Ltd., London.

CO = Columbia University, Butler Library, New York City.

CU = Cornell University, University Library, Ithaca.

D = Dartmouth College, Baker Memorial Library, Hanover.

H = William Heinemann, Ltd., London.

HL = The Huntington, Library, San Marino.

HU = Harvard University, Houghton Library, Cambridge.

IU = Indiana University, The Lilly Library, Bloomington.

LC = Library of Congress, Washington.

MC = Middlebury College, Abernathy Library, Middlebury.

NA = National Library of Australia, Canberra.

NE = The Newberry Library, Special Collections, Chicago.

NU = Northwestern University, The University Library, Evanston.

NYPL = New York Public Library, Berg Collection, New York City.

NYU = New York University, Libraries - Division of Special Collections, New York City.

P = Estate of Norman Holmes Pearson, c/o Yale University, New Haven.

SIU   =   Southern Illinois University, The Morris
          Library, Carbondale.

SU   =   Stanford University, Stanford University
          Libraries, Stanford.

SUNY =   State University of New York, The University
          Libraries, Buffalo.

T   =   F.-J. Temple, c/o O. R. T. F., Montpellier.

TU   =   Temple University, Manuscript Collection,
          Philadelphia.

UA   =   University of Arkansas, University Library,
          Fayetteville.

UB   =   University of Birmingham, University Library,
          Birmingham.

UC   =   University of Chicago, The Joseph Regenstein
          Library, Chicago.

UCB   =   University of California, The Bancroft Library,
          Berkeley.

UCLA =   University of California, University Research
          Library, Los Angeles.

UI   =   University of Iowa, University Libraries, Iowa
          City.

UIL   =   University of Illinois, University Library,
          Urbana.

UK   =   University of Kansas, Kenneth Spenser Research
          Library, Lawrence.

UL   =   University of London, University Library, London.

UP   =   University of Pennsylvania, University Libraries,
          Philadelphia.

UT   =   University of Texas, Humanities Research Center,
          Austin.

UTO   =   University of Toronto, University Library,
          Toronto.

UV   =   University of Virginia, Library, Charlottesville.

UVI   =   University of Victoria, Victoria.

UW   =   University of Washington, Libraries, Seattle.

V   =   Viking Press, Inc., New York City.

YU   =   Yale University, Beinecke Rare Book and
          Manuscript Library, New Haven.

YU-P =   Yale University, Beinecke Rare Book and
         Manuscript Library, Bequest of Norman Holmes
         Pearson, New Haven.

WU   =   Washington University, Libraries, St. Louis.

3

Abbreviations Used for Aldington's Principal Addresses

(An "address" does not always mean that Aldington resided there.)

Aix-en-Provence = Hotel de Sévigné, Rue de Bernardines, and elsewhere, Aix-en-Provence, France.

Authors' Club = The Authors' Club, 2 Whitehall Court, London, England.

BEF = British Expeditionary Forces in England and France.

Bloomsbury = Oakley House, Bloomsbury Street, London, England. (*The Egoist*)

Le Canadel = Villa Koeclin and elsewhere, Le Canadel, Var, France.

Corneille = Hotel Corneille, Rue Corneille, Paris, France.

Hampstead = 7 Christchurch Place, Hampstead, London, England.

Hermitage = Chapel Farm Cottage, Newbury, Berkshire, England.

Hollywood = 8439 Sunset Blvd. and elsewhere, Hollywood, California, U.S.

Jamaica = Chatham Hotel, Montego Bay, Jamaica, B.W.I.

Jamay = Jamay Beach, Nokomis, Florida, U.S.

Kensington = 8 Holland Place Chambers, Kensington, London, England.

Le Lavandou = Villa Aucassin, St. Clair, par Le Lavandou, Var, France.

Littoral = Hotel du Littoral, Ren St., London, England.

Mecklenburg Square = 44 Mecklenburg Square, London, England.

Montparnasse = 162 Boulevard Montparnasse, Paris, France.

Montpellier = Villa Les Rosiers, Ancien Chemin de Castlenau, Montpellier, Hérault, France.

New York City = 620 West 115th St., New York, N.Y., U.S.

Old Lyme = Brockway Manor and elsewhere, Old Lyme, Connecticut, U.S.

Padworth = Malthouse Cottage, Padworth near Reading,
    Berkshire, England.

Pramousquier = Villa Devos, Pramousquier par Le Lavandou,
    Var, France.

Raspail = Hotel L'Aiglon, Boulevard Raspail, Paris, France.

Rye = Mermaid Street, Rye, Sussex, England.

Saintes = Dromar, Les Saintes-Maries-de-la-Mer, Camargue,
    France.

St. James's St. = 4 Palace Place Chambers, 24 St. James's
    St., London, England.

Select = The Select, Place de la Sorbonne, Paris, France.

Sury = Chez Alister Kershaw, Maison Sallé, Sury-en-Vaux,
    Cher, France.

Tobago = Terry Hall, Mount St. George, Tobago, B.W.I.

Twickenham = Jesmond, London Road, Twickenham, England.

Ursulines = 14 Rue des Ursulines, Paris, France.

Washington = The Dupont Circle, Washington, D.C., U.S.

Woodland Cottage = Woodland Cottage, Martinhoe,
    Parracombe, North Devonshire, England.

4

Alphabetical Listing
of Letters by Recipients

Recipients' names are listed alphabetically. Single
letters (this term is also used for postcards, notes, etc.)
or groups of letters are arranged chronologically under
the recipient's name. First the number of letters is
given, then the date(s) for three (usually) or less or
the terminal dates for larger groups. Next follows a
description, then the place, and finally the repository.
Enclosures are listed last, and then only if of some
importance, and if they were inventoried by the
repository.

Abbreviations.

acs	=	autograph card signed
an	=	autograph note
ani	=	autograph note initialed
ans	=	autograph note signed
apci	=	autograph postcard initialed
apcs	=	autograph postcard signed
al	=	autograph letter
ali	=	autograph letter initialed
als	=	autograph letter signed
tl	=	typewritten letter
tli	=	typewritten letter initialed
tls	=	typewritten letter signed
n.d.	=	no date
n.p.	=	no place
[ ]	=	data included in brackets is derived indirectly
?	=	date is probably correct
+	=	enclosure

Aldington, Albert Edward (father); 21 letters

    3 - n.d. [May 1912] - apci, Paris, TU.

    2 - 20 and 23 May 1912 - apci, Paris, TU.

    1 - 12 December 1912 - apci, Rome, TU.

    3 - 18 and 22 March, 21 April 1913 - apci, Anacapri,
        TU.

    1 - 22 March 1913 - apci, Anacapri, SIU.

    2 - 2 and 6 May 1913 - apci, Florence, TU.

    3 - 7, 10 and 30 May 1913 - apci, Venice, TU.

    1 - 3 June 1913 - apci, Verona, TU.

    1 - 14 June 1913 - apci, Lago di Garda, TU.

    4 - 20 August 1913 to 9 May 1914 - apci, Kensington,
        TU.

Aldington, Margery and Patricia (sisters); 1 letter

    1 - 6 June 1912 - apci, Paris, TU.

Aldington, May (mother); 6 letters

    1 - 11 June 1912 - apci, Paris, TU.

    2 - 9 June 1912 (2) - apci, Paris, TU (message
        continued to second card).

    2 - 25 and 31 December 1912 - apci, Rome, TU.

    1 - 16 June 1913 - apci, Lago di Garda, TU.

Aldington, Miss (?); 1 letter

    1 - "Monday, 4:00 A.M." ["year 1913" holograph note]
        - apci, n.p. [card titled "Corfu Castle &
        Village"], TU.

Aldington, Miss and Mr. (?); 1 letter

    1 - 18 June 1912 - apci, Paris, TU.

Aldington, Netta (second wife, divorced from Michael
               Patmore; artist); 63 letters

   46 - 13 September 1951 to 5 May 1957 - tls,
        Montpellier, BM.

    1 - Palm Sunday, 1954 - tl, Montpellier, BM.

    1 - 12 May 1954 - tls, n.p. [Montpellier], BM.

11 - 19 May 1961 to 22 May 1962 - tls, Sury, BM.

1 - 7 December 1961 - tls, Aix-en-Provence, BM.

3 - 28 and 29 April, 22 May 1962 - tls, Sury,
recipient.

Aldington, P. A. G. (brother); 275 letters

5 - 20 September 1945 to 5 April 1946 - tls,
Hollywood, SIU.

4 - 22 April to 23 July 1946 - tls, Jamaica, SIU.

4 - 12 September to 12 October 1946 - tls, Raspail,
SIU.

8 - 31 January to 21 July 1947 - tls, Montparnasse,
SIU.

23 - 13 January 1948 to 29 March 1951 - tls, Le
Lavandou, SIU.

1 - 5 August 1949 - als, Paris, SIU.

79 - 8 July 1951 to 15 July 1957 - tls, Montpellier,
SIU, 8 October 1954 + two pp. suppressed
passages in *Death of a Hero;* 15 October 1954
+ newspaper clipping; 8 February 1956 + tls
Cockburn to Aldington.

1 - 7 April 1953 - als, Montpellier, SIU.

124 - 10 August 1957 to 22 July 1962 - tls, Sury, SIU,
20 December 1958 + copy of letter to Aldington
from Major Norman Bray of 2 July 1958.

1 - 2 May 1958 - tls, Sury, H.

2 - 2 July and 23 October 1960 - tls, "as from Sury
and Aix-en-Provence" [both Saintes], SIU.

1 - 22 January 1961 - tls, Aix-en-Provence, SIU.

1 - 30 January 1961 - apcs, Aix-en-Provence, SIU.

1 - 10 May 1961 - apcs, Venice, SIU.

18 - 3 October 1961 to 17 February 1962 - tls,
Aix-en-Provence, SIU.

1 - 30 June 1962 - apcs, n.p. [Leningrad], SIU.

1 - n.d. - tls, Le Lavandou, SIU.

Aldington, Patricia (sister); 4 letters

1 - 22 June 1935 - apc, New York City, TU.

1 - 28 December 1960 - apcs, Rome, TU.

1 - 25 March 1961 - apcs, Saintes, TU.

1 - 21 April 1961 - apcs, Venice, TU.

Aldis, Mrs. Arthur; 1 letter

1 - 22 December 1915 - als, Hampstead, NU.

American Express, Paris; 1 letter

1 - 1 February 1929 - tls, Rapallo, UT.

Arlott, John (writer, broadcaster, BBC producer,
          instructor for BBC Staff Training School);
          restricted; 2 letters

2 - 30 November 1944 and 6 November 1949 - tls,
    Le Lavandou, recipient.

Armstrong, Terence Tari Fytton (John Gawsworth - poet,
          essayist, bibliographer, editor, archivist);
          12 letters

1 - 24 October 1955 - tls, Montpellier, UT.

1 - 22 January 1961 - tls, Aix-en-Provence, UT, +
    petition to Trustees, Civil List Pension Fund,
    London, for widow of Philip Lindsay.

7 - 11 March 1961 to 26 July 1962 - tls, Sury, UT.

1 - n.d. [8 July 1961] - tl, n.p. [Sury], UT.

1 - 19 July 1961 - apci, Sury, UT.

1 - 26 July 1962 - tl (photocopy), Sury, SIU.

Atkins, John (critic, journalist, biographer); 15 letters

6 - 23 May to 5 December 1957 - tls, Montpellier, UT.

9 - 9 September 1957 to 2 May 1958 - tls, Sury, UT.

Bacon, Leonard (American poet); 223 letters

1 - 22 March 1931 - apcs, Cava [Italy], YU.

22 - 8 July 1935 to 17 October 1940 - tls, Old Lyme,
    YU.

1 - 9 September 1935 - als, Old Lyme, YU.

1 - 3 October 1935 - tls, London, YU.

2 - 17 July and 21 August 1936 - tls; Fernpass in
Tirol, Austria; YU.

9 - 16 November 1938 to 25 January 1939 - tls, Le
Canadel, YU.

1 - 7 February 1939 - als, London, YU.

3 - 19 February 1939, 3 and 12 August 1946 - als,
New York City, YU.

45 - 3 March 1939 to 9 June 1940 - tls, New York
City, YU.

9 - 15 November 1940 to 28 February 1941 - tls,
Washington, YU.

1 - 13 December 1940 - als, Washington, YU.

31 - 28 February 1941 to 8 November 1942 - tls,
Jamay, YU.

3 - 5, 20 and 26 June 1941 - tls; San Cristobal,
New Mexico; YU.

50 - 1 January 1943 to 26 March 1946 - tls, Hollywood,
YU.

1 - 19 September 1944 - tl, Hollywood, YU.

2 - 3 and 25 June 1946 - tls, Jamaica, YU.

4 - 14 September 1946 to 17 July 1947 - tls, Paris,
YU.

21 - 25 October 1947 to 13 April 1951 - tls, Le
Lavandou, YU.

14 - 21 March 1953 to 16 December 1954 - tls,
Montpellier, YU.

2 - 6 April 1953 and 3 June 1954 - als, Montpellier,
YU.

Barnes, M. W. (admirer of D. H. Lawrence from Nottingham,
England); 7 letters

7 - 14 June 1958 to 14 April 1960 - tls, Sury, UT.

Barrow, General Sir George de Symons (British army from
          1884 to 1929; in India, East Indies,
          Waziristan, China, etc.; writer); 1 letter
     1 - 12 February 1955 - tls, Montpellier, SIU.
Barton, Miss; 1 letter
     1 - 24 August 1930 - tls, Le Lavandou, SIU.
Beaumont, Cyril W. (bookseller, publisher, writer on
          ballet); 16 letters
     1 - 21 March 1918 - als, BEF (Newhaven), UI.
     1 - 30 March 1918 - als, BEF, UI
     1 - 31 March 1918 - als, BEF (Tunbridge Wells), UI.
     3 - 5 and 13 July, 29 December 1918 - als, n.p., UI.
     4 - 9 February to 12 May 1920 - als, Hermitage, UI.
     1 - 21 April 1920 - als; Hermitage; Professor Miriam
          J. Benkovitz, c/o Skidmore College, Saratoga
          Springs, New York.
     3 - 6 July and 6 December 1921, 16 January 1923 -
          als, Padworth, UI.
     1 - 20 July 1921 - apcs; Tewkesbury, England; UI.
     1 - 25 July 1921 - als; New Radnor, England; UI.
Berkhoff, Anita Engle (author of *The Nili Spies*); 3 letters
     3 - 26 August and 28 December (2) 1957 - tls, Sury,
          recipient.
Best, Marshall (Viking Press, Inc.); 57 letters
     1 - 4 May 1940 - tls, New York City, V.
     4 - 15 to 28 February 1941 - tls, Washington, V.
     27 - 7 March 1941 to 26 August 1942 - tls, Jamay, V,
          + a list of suggested features of the Poetry
          Anthology which should be emphasized in promotion.
     2 - 13 June and 22 July 1941 - tls; San Cristobal,
          New Mexico; V.
     1 - 21 July 1942 - tls; Boulder, Colorado; V.
     20 - 18 September 1942 to 10 October 1945 - tls,

Hollywood, V, + suggested writing projects:
prose anthology, biography of Wellington, and
an addition to his memoirs.

2 - 11 and 22 March 1947 - tls, Montparnasse, V.

Birch, R. D.; 1 letter

1 - 4 May 1955 - tls, Montpellier, SIU.

Bird, Alan (art historian, critic, lecturer - these letters
          have been published by Professor Miriam J.
          Benkovitz); 147 letters

12 - 3 February 1949 to 23 April 1951 - tls, Le
     Lavandou, NYPL.

117 - 10 June 1951 to 19 May 1957 - tls, Montpellier,
      NYPL.

1 - 13 August 1954 - tls; À Daou, Le Lavandou; NYPL.

16 - 2 January 1958 to 11 August 1961 - tls, Sury,
     NYPL.

1 - 5 February 1962 - tls, Aix-en-Provence, NYPL.

Blaber, Mr.; 1 letter

1 - "Friday" [1911] - als, n.p. [Twickenham], UT
    (on "D. Appleton & Company" letterhead).

Bonham-Carter, Hon Mark Raymond (a director of William
          Collins & Co.); 7 letters

3 - 30 September and 13 November 1954, 9 September
    1955 - tls, Montpellier, SIU.

4 - 21 October 1954 to 9 January 1957 - tl,
    Montpellier, SIU.

Bookishly (London publisher?); 1 letter

1 - 18 December 1908 - telegram, London, SIU.

Brady, Jack (editor, *Parnassus*); 1 letter

1 - 10 November 1923 - als, n.p. [written on
    Criterion letterhead], WU.

Brown, Edmund R. (Four Seas Company); 35 letters

4 - 13 July 1915 to 7 March 1920 - tls, London, NYU.

8 - 10 August 1915 to 26 May 1920 - als, London, NYU.

1 - 21 July 1917 - als, Mecklenburg Square, UW.

1 - 10 July 1918 - als, BEF, NYU.

3 - 17 March, 9 August and 11 September 1921 - als,
    Padworth, NYU.

2 - 13 June 1921 and 17 January 1923 - als, Padworth,
    TU.

1 - 9 November 1921 - als, Padworth, UW.

1 - 29 December 1923 - tls, Rome, NYU.

14 - 11 February 1924 to 24 January 1928 - tls,
    Padworth, NYU.

Browning, John (Evans Brothers Ltd., publishers); 1 letter

1 - 6 April 1951 - tl, Le Lavandou, SIU.

Bryher, Winifred (author of historical novels, published
                    Close-Up with Kenneth Macpherson;
                    companion of H. D., benefactor of
                    Catherine); 240 letters

3 - 22 September and 22 December 1918, 1 January 1919
    - als, BEF, P, + ms poem "Escape."

1 - 5 October 1918 - als, n.p., P, + ms poem "Faun
    Captive."

20 - 21 February 1953 to 20 July 1957 - tls,
    Montpellier, P.

1 - 8 April 1953 - als, Montpellier, P.

142 - 15 November 1958 to 24 July 1962 - tls, Sury, P.

1 - 16 July 1959 - tls; chez F.-J. Temple,
    Montpellier; P.

1 - 30 November 1959 - apci, Vézelay, P.

1 - 28 June 1960 - apci, Saintes, P.

11 - 1 July 1960 to 28 September 1961 - tls, Saintes, P.

1 - 3 August 1960 - apcs, Zagreb, P.

37 - 18 October 1960 to 24 February 1962 - tls,
    Aix-en-Provence, P.

1 - 21 December 1960 - als, Rome, P.

10 - 4 April to 16 May 1961 - als, Venice, P.

7 - 17 April to 12 May 1961 - apcs, Venice, P.

1 - 23 September 1961 - apcs, Saintes, P.

1 - 25 December [*sic* but must be June] 1962 - apcs, Moscow, P.

1 - 4 July 1962 - apcs, Moscow, P.

Bubb, Rev. Charles C. (proprietor of The Clerk's Press); 18 letters

1 - 19 June 1916 - als, Woodland Cottage, UCLA.

1 - n.d. - als, Mecklenburg Square, UCLA.

12 - 22 June 1917 to 14 April 1918 - als, Mecklenburg Square, UCLA.

1 - 12 July 1918 - als, BEF, UCLA.

1 - 8 December 1918 - als, n.p., UCLA.

1 - 21 February 1919 - als, Rye, UCLA.

1 - 27 February 1919 - als, Author's Club, UCLA.

Buck, Mitchell S.; 3 letters

1 - 18 February 1916 - tls, Bloomsbury, NYPL.

1 - 7 July 1921 - als, Padworth, UP.

1 - 2 August 1921 - als, Padworth, NYPL.

Burke, Mr.; 1 letter

1 - 23 August 1958 - tls, Sury, SIU.

Callender, Miss L. (William Heinemann, Ltd.); 2 letters

2 - 6 November and 21 December 1948 - tls, Le Lavandou, H.

Campbell, Mary (wife of the poet Roy Campbell); 2 letters

1 - [?] - tls, Montpellier, recipient.

1 - 1 May 1959 - tls, Sury, recipient.

Campbell, Roy (poet); 8 letters

3 - 6 October 1953, 3 November 1956 and [?] - tls, Montpellier, Mrs. Mary Campbell.

4 - 5 July to 12 September 1954 - tls, Montpellier,

NYPL.

   1 - 18 August 1954 - tls, Le Lavandou, Mrs. Mary
     Campbell.

Cape, Jonathan (Jonathan Cape, Ltd., publishers);
       1 letter

   1 - 26 February 1933 - tls, St. James's Street, C.

Cate, Garth; 1 letter

   1 - 12 June 1935 - tls, n.p. [New York City], SIU.
     (Copy at UCLA.)

Church, Richard (English writer of poetry, autobiography,
          novels, essays. Participated in
             establishing *Criterion*); 11 letters

   1 - 17 September 1923 - tls, Padworth, UT (on *The*
    Criterion letterhead).

   2 - 22 September and 11 October 1923 - als, Padworth,
    UT.

   1 - 19 February 1933 - tls, St. James's Street, UT.

   1 - 11 May 1935 - tls, Tobago, UT.

   1 - 27 June 1935 - tls, New York City, UT.

   2 - 6 October and 2 December 1946 - tls, Raspail, UT.

   3 - 30 March, 6 and 14 December 1954 - tls, Montpellier,
    UT.

Cockburn, Frank B. (of Horne and Birkett, Aldington's
          attorneys); 6 letters

   4 - 30 September 1954 to 12 October 1955 - tls,
    Montpellier, SIU.

   1 - 25 October 1954 - tl, Paris, SIU.

   1 - 14 December 1954 - tl, Montpellier, SIU.

Coghill, [?]; 1 letter

   1 - 23 January 1936 - tls; Cavendish Hotel, Jermyn St.,
    London; SIU.

Collins, William (publishers); 4 letters

   2 - 6 February and 8 September 1952 - tls, Montpellier,

SIU.

2 - 2 February 1953 and 22 February 1954 - tl,
Montpellier, SIU.

Constable & Company (publishers); 3 letters

3 - [ca. June or July 1915], 10, 20 August 1915 -
tls, Hampstead, TU.

Cournos, John (Russian-born naturalized American, journalist,
translator; early friend of Aldington who
lived in the same house in Mecklenburg Square,
London); 34 letters

1 - n.d. - ans, n.p., HU.

1 - "Tuesday" - tls, Corneille, HU.

11 - [July 1916] to 6 April 1918 - als, BEF, HU.

3 - 29 August to 10 September 1929 - tls; Hotel Rivage
de Fabrégas, Fabrégas, La Seyne, Var, France; HU.

2 - 17 and 19 September 1929 - tls, Corneille, HU.

1 - 22 November 1929 - tls, Rome, HU.

4 - 5 December 1929 to 27 November 1930 - tls; c/o
Barclays Bank, Paris [Amalfi, etc., Italy], HU.

1 - 23 December 1929 - tls; c/o Cooks, Palermo,
Italy; HU.

1 - 11 February 1930 - apci; Touggourt, Algeria; HU.

2 - 28 May and 18 June 1930 - tls, Ursulines, HU.

1 - 25 March 1931 - acs, Rome, HU.

1 - 28 May 1931 - tls, Le Canadel, HU.

1 - 20 August 1932 - tls, Capri, HU.

1 - 13 February 1933 - tls, St. James's St., HU.

1 - 30 July 1933 - tls, c/o Chatto & Windus [written
from the south of France], HU.

1 - 18 August 1933 - tls, Pramousquier, HU.

1 - 5 May 1934 - tls, c/o Chatto & Windus, London; HU.

Covici, Pascal (Chicago publisher later associated with
the Viking Press, Inc.); 39 letters

1 - 19 December 1924 - tls, Padworth, YU.

1 - 31 August 1927 - als, Padworth, UT, + "complete
   illustrations for Gourmont anthology."

3 - 31 January, 2 and 29 February 1940 - tls, New
   York City, V.

1 - 4 October 1940 - tls, Old Lyme, V.

9 - 20 November 1940 to 20 January 1941 - tls,
   Washington, V.

4 - 24 March 1941 to 2 March 1942 - tls, Jamay, V.

1 - 1 September 1946 - tls; c/o American Express, Rue
   Scribe, Paris; V.

4 - 27 June 1948 to 11 February 1950 - tls, Le
   Lavandou, V.

1 - 22 September 1951 - tls, Montpellier, UT.

6 - 19 August 1952 to 27 June 1955 - tls, Montpellier,
   V.

5 - 9 January 1958 to 5 May 1959 - tls, Sury, V.

3 - 28 January 1958, 20 February 1961 and 19 July
   1962 - tls, Sury, UT, 20 February 1961 + the
   Milissa Press edition of *A Tourist's Rome*, 19 July
   1962 + translation of address by Pavel Chuvikov
   given 8 July 1962.

Cunard, Nancy (poet, journalist, publisher); 1 letter

1 - 1 February 1929 - tls, Rapallo, UT.

Dahlberg, Edward (American novelist and essayist); 10 letters

3 - 30 July 1950, 12 September and 3 February 1951 -
   tls, Le Lavandou, UT.

7 - 22 October 1954 to 16 July 1956 - tls, Montpellier,
   UT.

Davis, Lambert (editor, *Virginia Quarterly Review*);
         1 letter

1 - 25 September 1934 - tls; c/o Ralph Pinker,
   London; UV.

Deasey, W. Denison (Australian historian, friend of Kershaw;
                did research for Aldington on T. E.
                Lawrence at the British Museum); 161
                letters

  24 - 17 January 1949 to 20 April 1951 - tls, Le
       Lavandou, NA.

   1 - 10 December 1949 - tl, Le Lavandou, NA.

   1 - 12 March 1951 - tls, Le Lavandou, recipient.

   1 - 10 April 1951 - als, Le Lavandou, NA.

 118 - 28 May 1951 to 3 May 1957 - tls, Montpellier, NA.

   2 - 4 August 1952 and 21 August 1955 - tl, Montpellier,
       NA.

   1 - 30 March 1953 - apcs, Le Lavandou, recipient.

   1 - 1 April 1953 - als, Le Lavandou, NA.

   2 - 19 July and 17 October 1955 - tls, Montpellier,
       recipient.

   9 - 12 January 1958 to 1 February 1960 - tls, Sury, NA.

   1 - 23 April 1960 - tls, Sury, recipient.

Dibben, William (English civil servant; bibliophile;
                located hard-to-find books for Aldington);
                201 letters

  75 - 28 October 1947 to 22 April 1951 - tls, Le
       Lavandou, Collection of Raymond and Peggy Sturge,
       Bournemouth, England.

  46 - 5 June 1951 to 11 April 1954 - tls, Montpellier,
       Collection of Raymond and Peggy Sturge,
       Bournemouth, England.

   2 - 17 and 21 April 1954 - tls; À Daou, par Le
       Lavandou, Var; Collection of Raymond and Peggy
       Sturge, Bournemouth, England.

  78 - 24 May 1954 to 21 August 1956 - tls, Montpellier,
       Collection of Raymond and Peggy Sturge,
       Bournemouth, England.

Dobrée, Mrs. Bonamy (Valentine, wife of the critic, editor,
              literary scholar and professor at
              Leeds University); 1 letter
    1 - "June 1929" - tls, La Rochelle, YU-P.
Doolittle, Hilda (H. D., Aldington's first wife, poet,
              novelist); 716 letters
    1 - n.d. - tls, n.p., YU-P.
    1 - n.d. - ali; 52 Doughty St., London; YU-P.
    1 - "Tuesday" - tls, Hotel Grande Bretagne, YU-P.
    1 - "Tuesday" - tls, Select, YU-P.
    1 - "Weds" - als, Littoral, YU-P.
   76 - 6 January 1918 to 29 January 1919 - als, BEF,
        YU-P, 27 July 1918 + version of poem "Faun
        Captive"; autograph copy of "Prayers and Fantasies
        I-VIII" dated "France 1918"; postcard photographs
        of R. A. and his group in dress and battle
        uniforms (15 June 1918); also photo of R. A.
        alone, 8 July 1918 + poem; 26 June 1918 letter
        from C. W. Beaumont; group photograph of R. A.
        in uniform dated 8 August 1918; letter 20 July
        1918 + poem; copy of poem "Epilogue" ("War Bones"
        crossed out) beginning "Eleven years after. . . ."
    1 - 9 January 1918 - ali, BEF, YU-P.
    2 - 11 and 31 May 1918 - apcs, BEF, YU-P.
    3 - 2, 13 and 21 January 1919 - als, n.p., YU-P.
    2 - "Thursday" and 24 February 1919 - als, Littoral,
        YU-P.
    1 - 1 March 1919 - als; 52 Doughty St., London; YU-P.
    2 - 5 and 26 April 1919 - als, Author's Club, YU-P.
    1 - 28 January 1920 - ali, Hermitage, YU-P.
    1 - 14 March 1929 - tls; c/o Barclays Bank, Paris;
        YU-P.
   12 - 20 March to 9 June 1929 - tls, Select, YU-P.

1 - 3 April 1929 - tls, n.p., YU-P.

2 - 14 April and 25 May 1929 - als, Select, YU-P.

2 - 11 and 19 June 1929 - tls; Notre-Dame Hotel, Quai
Saint Michael; YU-P.

3 - 30 June, 7 and 13 July 1929 - tls; Hotel des
Flots, Chatelaillon-Plage, Charente-Infèrieure;
YU-P.

1 - 15 July 1929 - tli, n.p. YU-P.

6 - 27 July to 12 September 1929 - tls; Hotel Rivage
de Fabrégas, Fabrégas, La Seyne, Var; YU-P.

1 - 1 October 1929 - tls, Corneille, YU-P.

2 - 5 December 1929 and 27 November 1930 - tls; c/o
Barclays Bank, Paris; YU-P, + account to 26
November of *Imagist Anthology 1930* enclosed with
letter of 27 November 1930.

1 - 10 January 1930 - tls; c/o Cook's Tunis; YU-P.

1 - 20 January 1930 - apci; Gabes, Tunisia; YU-P.

1 - 23 February 1930 - tls; c/o Barclays Bank, Paris
[Algeria]; YU-P.

3 - 2 and 25 May, 23 June 1930 - tls, Ursulines, YU-P.

1 - 11 July 1930 - tls; Le Bouguet, Aigrebelle, par Le
Lavandou, Var; YU-P.

1 - 1 December 1930 - tls, Lecce, YU-P.

3 - 16 December, 13 February, 17 March 1931 - tls;
c/o Cook's Florence; YU-P.

4 - 5 June 1931 to 24 February 1938 - tls, Le Canadel,
YU-P.

1 - 21 February 1932 - tls, n.p., YU-P.

1 - 24 June 1938 - tls; Astor Hotel, Prince's Square,
[London]; YU-P.

2 - 20 July and 9 August 1939 - tls; The Scallop
Shell, Peace Dale, R.I.; YU-P.

3 - 4 September, 13 October and 29 November 1939 -

tls; c/o Viking Press, Inc., New York City; YU-P.

1 - 30 April 1942 - tls, Jamay, YU-P.

2 - 14 February 1945 and 23 January 1946 - tls,
Hollywood, YU-P.

7 - 25 September to 11 December 1946 - tls, Raspail;
YU-P.

18 - 18 January to 25 July 1947 - tls, Montparnasse,
YU-P, + typed lines from Morris's "Golden Wings"
with 10 June 1947.

64 - 7 August 1947 to 9 March 1951 - tls, Le Lavandou,
YU-P.

190 - 29 May 1951 to 20 July 1957 - tls, Montpellier,
YU-P, + "saga" of T. E. Lawrence book with letter
of 2 September 1953.

6 - 28 June 1951 to 1 July 1959 - apcs, Montpellier,
YU-P.

1 - 4 February 1953 - als, "as from Montpellier" [St.
Clair], YU-P.

1 - 26 March 1953 - apcs, Avignon, YU-P.

1 - 30 March 1953 - apcs; À Doau, St. Clair, par Le
Lavandou, Var; YU-P.

1 - 18 August 1953 - apcs, La Camargue [Montpellier],
YU-P.

1 - 22 April 1954 - tls, Le Lavandou, YU-P.

1 - 17 May 1957 - apci, Montpellier, YU-P.

1 - 25 July 1957 - apcs, Riom, YU-P.

3 - 27 and 28 July, 2 August 1957 - apci, Sancerre,
YU-P.

195 - 22 August 1957 to 27 March 1961 - tls, Sury,
YU-P, + 28 January 1960 letter from M. Urnov to
R. A.; letter 7 November 1960 + annotated copy
of Megata's essay on R. A.

1 - 1 January 1959 - apci, Monaco, YU-P.

   3 - 3, 10 and 18 July 1959 - tls; chez F.-J. Temple,
       Montpellier; YU-P.

   1 - 30 November 1959 - apci, Velézay, YU-P.

  10 - 24 June 1960 to 8 April 1961 - tls, Saintes, YU-P.

   3 - 26 and 28 June, 1 July 1960 - apci, Saintes, YU-P.

  13 - 23 October 1960 to 2 February 1961 - tls, Aix-en-
       Provence, YU-P.

   2 - 24 October and 2 December 1960 - apcs, Aix-en-
       Provence, YU-P.

   4 - 25 October 1960 to 22 March 1961 - apci, Aix-en-
       Provence, YU-P.

   2 - 19 and 28 December 1960 - apcs, Rome, YU-P.

   1 - 23 December 1960 - als, Rome, YU-P.

   1 - 24 December 1960 - apci, Rome, YU-P.

   1 - 14 March 1961 - apcs, Orange, YU-P.

   1 - 14 March 1961 - apci, Orange, YU-P.

   2 - 17 March 1961 (2) - apci, Saintes, YU-P.

  15 - 17 March to 12 May 1961 - apci, Venice, YU-P.

   9 - 4 April to 13 May 1961 - als, Venice, YU-P.

   1 - 13 April 1961 - apci, Cannes, YU-P.

   2 - 15 and 16 April 1961 - apcs, Venice, YU-P.

   1 - 12 May 1961 - als, "as from Mas Dromar" [Venice],
       YU-P.

   2 - 19 and 23 May 1961 - tls, "as from Sury" [Saintes],
       YU-P.

   2 - 1 and 8 June 1961 - tls, Sury, YU-P.

Doran, George H. (American publisher); 3 letters

   3 - 19, 21, and 24 May 1927 - tl, carbon copies,
       Padworth, YU.

Douglas, Robin (son of Norman Douglas?); 1 letter

   1 - 7 April 1941 - tls, Jamay, UCLA.

Drake, Lawrence; 6 letters

   5 - 30 May to 13 September 1931 - tls, le Canadel, SIU.

1 - 2 March 1933 - tls, n.p., SIU.

Dujardin, Édouard (French writer; an associate of George
                Moore?); 1 letter

1 - 21 June 1920 - als, Authors' Club, SUNY.

Durrell, Lawrence (English foreign service officer; poet,
                author of *Alexandria Quartet);* 197
                letters

1 - 8 September 1933 - tls; c/o Chatto & Windus,
   London; SIU.

20 - 1 February to 17 July 1957 - tls, Montpellier, SIU.

126 - 24 August 1957 to 26 July 1962 [the last letter was
   written the day before Aldington's death] - tls,
   Sury, SIU.

1 - 27 July 1959 - apcs, Montpellier, SIU.

1 - 27 November 1959 - apcs, Zurich, SIU.

2 - 4 July 1960 and 31 March 1961 - tls, Saintes, SIU.

2 - 23 and 25 October 1960 - tls, Aix-en-Provence, SIU.

1 - 30 October 1960 - tls, "Sury (in fact Camargue),"
   SIU.

3 - 2 and 23 November, 5 December 1960 - apcs, Aix-
   en-Provence, SIU.

1 - 30 November 1960 - apcs, Sancerre, SIU.

28 - 7 December 1960 to 25 February 1962 - tls,
   Aix-en-Provence, SIU.

5 - 16 March to 17 May 1961 - apcs, Venice, SIU.

1 - 27 March 1961 - tls, Saintes, SIU.

1 - 7 May 1961 - als, Venice, SIU.

1 - 23 May 1961 - tls, "as from Sury," SIU.

1 - 22 June 1961 - apcs, Sury, SIU.

2 - 25 June and 4 July 1962 - apcs, Moscow, SIU.

Dutton, G. P. H. and Ninette Dutton (author; lecturer in
                English; Adelaide, S.A.); 220 letters

220 (approx.) - 1954 to 1962 - nearly all tls;

Montpellier, Aix-en-Provence, Sury; recipient.

Dyson, Mr.; 2 letters

    1 - 8 July 1931 - tls, Le Canadel, SIU.

    1 - 25 September 1934 - tl, Perpignan, SIU.

Eastman, Max (American author; translator, editor,
           anthologist, essayist; once edited *Masses*);
           1 letter

    1 - 3 August 1941 - tls, Jamay, IU.

Editor, *Atlantic Monthly*; 1 letter

    1 - 12 December 1955 - tl, Montpellier, SIU.

Editor, *Daily Telegram*; 1 letter

    1 - 2 March 1955 - tl (carbon), Montpellier, NYPL.

Editor, *Montreal Gazette*; 3 letters

    3 - 9 and 21 January, 1 February 1956 - tls,
        Montpellier, SIU.

Editor, *The Nation*; 1 letter

    1 - 14 July 1956 - tls, Montpellier, SIU.

Eisenberg, Miss (Viking Press, Inc.); 1 letter

    1 - 11 December 1940 - tls, Washington, V.

Eliot, T. S. (poet, critic, editor, publisher); 12 letters

    1 - "Tuesday 23" - als; "15 Mon. St W." [15
       Montague St., London]; HU.

    1 - 18 July 1919 - als, Authors' Club, HU.

    8 - 21 December 1919 to 26 November 1920 - als,
        Hermitage, HU.

    1 - "Wednesday" [1920] - als, Hermitage, HU.

    1 - 11 January 1921 - als, Padworth, HU.

Evans, A. Dwye (William Heinemann, LTd.); 1 letter

    1 - 2 September 1956 - tls, Montpellier, H.

Evans, C. S. (William Heinemann, Ltd.); 4 letters

    1 - 22 December 1936 - als, S. S. *Normandie*, H.

    1 - 20 February 1937 - tls, Florence, H.

    1 - 31 October 1937 - tls; Pinner Hill, Middlesex; H.

1 - 5 November 1937 - tls; Ashley Bank, Pinner
    Hill, Middlesex; H.

Fanchette, Jean (editor of *Two Cities*); 5 letters

    5 - 17 January to 10 April 1959 - tls, Sury, UK.

Fitzgerald, V. F. (University of Washington Bookstore,
                Seattle); 1 letter

    1 - 29 April 1928 - tls, Padworth, UT.

Flanner, Janet (American journalist who lived in Paris
        and wrote for the *New Yorker* as Gênet;
        novelist, translator); 1 letter

    1 - 1 February 1929 - tls, Rapallo, UT.

Fletcher, John Gould (American poet; Imagist); 9 letters

    7 - 9 August 1925 to 10 March 1927 - tls, Padworth,
    UA.

    1 - 12 August 1927 - als, Padworth, UA.

    1 - 30 April 1929 - tls, Paris, UA.

Flint, Frank Stewart (English Imagist poet, essayist,
                translator); 239 letters

    3 - n.d. - ali (in French), n.p., UT.

    1 - n.d. - tli, n.p., UT.

    1 - n.d. - ali, Bloomsbury, UT.

    1 - "Tuesday" - ali, n.p., UT.

    1 - "Sat." - tls, n.p., UT.

    1 - "Tuesday" - tli (in French), Hermitage, UT.

    1 - "Wednesday" - ali, Hermitage, UT.

    1 - "Wednesday" - tls, Padworth, UT.

    1 - "Wednesday" - ali, Padworth, UT.

    4 - n.d. [one "Wed."] - apci, n.p., UT.

    1 - "Sunday" - apci, n.p., UT.

    1 - "Thursday" - [10 April 19?] - als, n.p. [London],
    UT.

    1 - "Saturday" [7 December 1912] - als, n.p. [London],
    UT.

10 - 4 September to 21 November 1913 - tls,
     Kensington, UT.

1 - 29 October 1913 - als, Kensington, UT.

2 - n.d. [24 November and 3 December 1913] - apci,
    n.p. [Kensington], UT.

2 - n.d. [6 and 9 December 1913] - tls (in French),
    n.p. [Kensington] (on letterhead of *The New
    Freewoman*), UT.

1 - n.d. [11 December 1913] - als, n.p. [Kensington]
    (on the letterhead of *The New Freewoman*), UT.

1 - n.d. [15 December 1913] - ani, n.p. [Kensington],
    UT.

1 - n.d. [20 December 1913] - ali, Kensington (on the
    letterhead of *The New Freewoman*), UT.

1 - n.d. [31 December 1913] - ali, Bloomsbury (on the
    letterhead of *The New Freewoman*), UT.

5 - 8 January to [7 July 1914] - apci, Kensington,
    UT.

4 - 12 January to [16 October] 1914 - tls,
    Kensington, UT.

1 - "Monday" [11 May 1914] - als, Kensington, UT.

1 - n.d. [17 June 1914] - als, n.p. [London], UT.

1 - n.d. [8 July 1914] - als, Kensington, UT.

1 - 19 October 1914 - als, London, UT.

1 - 30 December 1914 - als, Bloomsbury, UT.

1 - n.d. [14 January 1915] - ali, Bloomsbury, UT.

1 - n.d. [8 February 1915] - als, Hampstead, UT.

3 - 8 February, 7 April and 15 September 1915 - als,
    Hampstead, UT.

1 - n.d. [22 February 1915] - tli, Hampstead, UT.

2 - n.d. [15 March and 5 April 1915] - ali,
    Hampstead, UT.

1 - n.d. [7 April 1915] - als, Hampstead, UT.

1 - 16 June 1915 - als; Daisy Meadow, Brasted, Kent;
    UT.

1 - n.d. [10 August 1915] - apci, n.p. [Hampstead],
    UT.

2 - 11 August and 2 September 1915 - tls, Hampstead,
    UT.

1 - 8 September 1915 - ali, n.p., UT.

1 - 14 September 1915 - als, Bloomsbury, UT.

1 - 23 October 1915 - ali, n.p. [London], UT.

1 - 9 December 1915 - apci, n.p. [Hampstead], UT.

1 - n.d. [25 December 1915] - apci, n.p., UT.

1 - n.d. - ali, BEF, UT.

1 - 3 January 1916 - ali, BEF, UT.

2 - 14 January and 8 February 1916 - ali, Hampstead,
    UT.

6 - 6 March to 9 May 1916 - ali, Woodland Cottage, UT.

1 - 21 March 1916 - als; BEF (Wareham, Dorset); UT.

2 - n.d. [24 March 1916] and 5 May 1916 - apci,
    Woodland Cottage, UT.

1 - 9 May 1916 - als, Woodland Cottage, UT.

1 - 26 May 1916 - ali, Woodland Cottage, UT.

1 - 2 June 1916 - ali, n.p., UT.

1 - 12 June 1916 - als, Woodland Cottage, UT.

2 - 25 June and 10 July 1916 - apci; BEF (Wareham,
    Dorset); UT.

3 - 13, 20 and 24 July 1916 - ali; BEF (Wareham,
    Dorset); UT.

2 - 16 July and 9 August 1916 - ali, n.p., UT.

1 - 17 August 1916 - ali; BEF (Worgret Camp, Poole); UT.

1 - 15 September 1916 - apci; BEF (Worgret Camp,
    Poole); UT.

1 - "Monday" [6 November 1916] - ali; BEF (Weymouth,
    Dorset); UT.

1 - 12 November 1916 - als; BEF (Weymouth, Dorset);
     UT.

2 - 15 November and 20 December 1916 - ali; BEF
     (Portland, Dorset); UT.

1 - 19 November 1916 - ali, BEF, UT.

1 - 1 December 1916 - ali, n.p., UT.

1 - n.d. [4 January 1917] - ali (in French), n.p.
     [BEF], UT.

3 - 13 and 22 January, 3 March 1917 - als, n.p.
     [BEF, France], UT.

6 - 29 January to 20 April 1917 - ali, BEF [France], UT.

3 - 17 February, 21 March and 12 April 1917 - field
     service postcards, BEF [France], UT.

1 - n.d. [7 September 1917] - ali, BEF (Lichfield),
     UT.

1 - 28 December 1917 - als; BEF (Newhaven, Sussex);
     UT.

9 - 2 June to 27 October 1918 - als, BEF (Army Post
     Office), UT.

20 - 18 January 1919 to 16 March 1920 - ali, Hermitage,
     UT.

11 - 27 March to 25 August 1919 - als, Authors' Club,
      UT.

3 - 17 April, 11 and 17 May 1919 - als, Littoral, UT.

2 - 16 June and [23 July] 1919 - ali, Authors' Club,
     UT.

1 - 2 July 1919 - tls, Authors' Club, UT.

1 - n.d. [2 September 1919] - ali, Littoral, UT.

2 - n.d. [24 February] and 26 February 1920 - al,
     Hermitage, UT.

2 - 14 and 16 April 1920 - als, Hermitage, UT.

1 - 26 April 1920 - tls, Hermitage, UT.

1 - n.d. [9 July 1920] - ani on first page of proofs

of "The Art of Poetry," n.p., UT.

1 - n.d. [28 July 1920] - apci, Hermitage, UT.

2 - 17 August and 15 September 1920 - als,
    Hermitage, UT.

14 - 16 January 1921 to 14 May 1924 - ali, Padworth,
    UT.

7 - 1 March 1921 to 4 March 1923 - als, Padworth, UT.

3 - 12 July 1921 to 1 December 1924 - apci, n.p.
    [Beenham], UT.

2 - 27 October 1921 and 2 May 1922 - ali, n.p., UT.

4 - 29 October 1921 to n.d. [17 April 1923] - ali,
    n.p. [Beenham], UT.

14 - 27 January 1922 to 5 February 1925 - tli,
    Padworth, UT.

2 - 13 March 1922 and 28 April 1924 - tli, n.p.
    [Beenham, Reading], UT.

3 - 8, 19 and 21 September 1922 - apci, Rome, UT.

8 - 20 December 1922 to 21 December 1924 - tls,
    Padworth, UT.

3 - 12 January, 4 August and 3 October 1923 - apci,
    n.p. [Beenham], UT.

2 - 5 and 8 June 1923 - tls, n.p. [Beenham], UT.

1 - 28 August 1923 - apci, Padworth, UT.

1 - n.d. [12 September 1923] - apci, n.p. [Thatoham,
    Newbury], UT.

1 - 13 January 1924 - tls, Rome, UT.

1 - 1 May 1924 - ali, Rome, UT.

1 - 4 December 1924 - tli, n.p., UT.

Flint, Ruth (second wife of Frank Stewart Flint); 2
            letters

2 - 14 and 20 September 1923 - als, Padworth, UT.

Flint, Violet (first wife of Frank Stewart Flint); 2
            letters

1 - 11 July 1919 - als, Authors' Club, UT.

1 - 18 March 1920 - als, Hermitage, UT.

Frere, A. S. (editor, William Heinemann, Ltd.); 269
           letters

   1 - 12 August 1946 - tls, New York, H.

   1 - 6 September 1946 - tls, Paris, H.

   1 - n.d. [13 July 1947] - telegram, Paris, H.

   1 - 13 July 1947 - tls, Montparnasse, H.

 37 - 16 September 1947 to 12 September 1950 - tls,
     Le Lavandou, H.

   1 - 11 October 1951 - tls, Montpellier, SIU.

214 - 25 April 1952 to 13 July 1957 - tls,
     Montpellier, H.

   3 - 5 to 12 July 1952 - tls; La Falaise, St. Clair, Le
     Lavandou; H.

   1 - 30 March 1953 - als; À Daou, St. Clair, par Le
     Lavandou, Var; H.

   1 - 28 January 1954 - als, Montpellier, H.

   7 - 21 October 1957 to 27 February 1960 - tls, Sury, H.

   1 - 31 October 1960 - tl copy, Sury, SIU.

Gaige, Crosby (American publisher; theatrical producer;
         writer, editor, broadcaster); 28 letters

 14 - 20 April 1926 to 9 December 1927 - tls, Padworth,
     YU.

   1 - 28 December 1926 - apcs; The Cottage, Mouldstone
     Down, Combemartin, North Devon; YU.

   1 - 12 January 1927 - als, Padworth, YU.

   1 - 10 April 1927 - als; c/o Barclays Bank, Paris;
     YU.

   1 - 1 June 1927 - tls, Padworth, YU.

   1 - 10 October 1928 - tl completed als; La Vigie,
     Ile de Port-Cros, Var; YU.

   2 - "28/19/28" [*sic* but probably 28 October 1928]

and 14 November 1928 - tls; La Vigie, Ile de
Port-Cros, Var; YU.

6 - 1 December 1928 to 9 June 1929 - tls; c/o
Barclays Bank, Paris [Select]; YU.

1 - "August 1933" - tls; c/o Ralph Pinker, London; YU.

Gamble, Peter (Lawrence scholar?); 1 letter

1 - 16 January 1938 - Le Canadel, UT.

Garnett, David (Nonesuch Press; novelist and writer of
autobiography); 6 letters

6 - 27 November 1949 to 9 July 1950 - tls, Le
Lavandou, UT.

Gawsworth, John

(See Armstrong, Terence Tari Fytton.)

Gilbert, Margery Lyon (sister); 39 letters

4 - 4 June to 29 June 1912 - apci, Paris, TU.

3 - 16 December 1912, 3 and 7 May 1913 - apcs,
Florence, TU.

3 - 28 December 1912, 7 and 19 September 1922 - apci,
Rome, TU.

1 - 24 March 1913 - apcs, Anacapri, SIU.

2 - 10 May 1913 and 9 October 1930 - apcs, Venice,
TU.

2 - 7 and 25 June 1913 - apci, Lago di Garda, TU.

1 - 30 October 1930 - apci, Venice, TU, photograph
of Aldington.

2 - 20 November and 11 December 1934 - tls; c/o
Chatto & Windus London; TU.

1 - 16 May 1935 - tls, Tobago, TU.

1 - 18 September 1936 - apcs; Brantôme, Dordogne; TU.

15 - 6 November 1959 to 13 July 1962 - tls, Sury, TU.

1 - 27 December 1960 - apcs, Rome, TU.

2 - 19 December 1961 and 25 January 1962 - tls, Aix-
en-Provence, TU.

1 - 30 June 1962 - apcs, Leningrad, TU.

Glass, Douglas; 1 letter

    1 - 11 September 1929 - tls; c/o Barclays Bank,
        Paris; SIU, + two photographs of Aldington.

Gosse, Sir Edmund (poet, biographer, critic, librarian);
        1 letter

    1 - 11 November 1927 - als, Padworth, UW.

Gribble, George (English playwright who lived in France);
        1 letter

    1 - 28 September 1925 - tls, Padworth, Mr. Guy Gribble.

Gribble, Guy (son of George Gribble; in Belgian foreign
        service?); 3 letters

    2 - 11 December 1958 and 17 February 1959 - tls, Sury,
        recipient.

    1 - 6 January 1961 - tls, Aix-en-Provence, recipient.

Guerard, Albert Leon (critic; literary historian; professor
        at Stanford 1926-1946); 1 letter

    1 - 26 November 1926 - tls, Padworth, SU.

Guillaume, Catherine Aldington (daughter); 1 letter

    1 - 26 December 1956 - apcs, Montpellier, SIU.

Guinzburg, Harold (Viking Press, Inc.); 26 letters

    1 - 10 August 1938 - tls; c/o Heinemann, London; V.

    2 - 16 September and 14 November 1938 - tls, Le
        Canadel, V.

    3 - 17 and 23 May, 8 June 1939 - tls; Crowfield,
        Saunderstown, Rhode Island; V.

   12 - 21 January to 26 April 1940 - tls, New York
        City, V.

    3 - 23 June, 26 August and 11 October 1940 - tls,
        Old Lyme, V, 23 June 1940 + copy tls 5 June
        1940 from A. S. Frere.

    3 - 20 March, 24 May 1941 and 2 January 1942 - tls,
        Jamay, V.

2 - 3 and 17 June 1941 - tls; c/o Frieda Lawrence,
    Kiowa Ranch, San Cristobal, New Mexico; V.

Haley, Sir William (editor London *Times* 1952 to 1966);
                    1 letter

"Letters cannot yet be assembled."

1 - 14 May 1954 - tl (carbon); c/o William Heinemann,
    Ltd., London; NYPL.

Hall, H. L. (William Heinemann, Ltd.); 2 letters

1 - 15 February 1948 - tls, Le Lavandou, SIU.

1 - 8 October 1948 - tls, Le Lavandou, H.

Hanley, James (novelist, essayist, short story writer);
                    8 letters

3 - 23 October, 4 and 11 November 1929 - tls; c/o
    Barclays Bank, Paris; SIU + two photographs of
    Aldington.

1 - 19 November 1929 - apcs, Rome, UK.

2 - 10 and 20 December 1929 - tls, Palermo, SIU.

1 - 5 February 1930 - tls; c/o Barclays Bank, Paris
    [Tunis]; UK.

1 - 3 April 1930 - als, Paris, UK.

Harald, Michael (wrote literary articles for Sir Oswald
                Mosley's weekly paper *Action*); 9 letters

8 - 31 January 1959 to 26 November 1960 - tls; Sury;
    Professor Miriam J. Benkovitz, c/o Skidmore
    College, Saratoga Springs, New York; 31 January
    1959 + copy of printed flyer re Prix Frédéric
    Mistral, and typed copy of part having to do with
    RA; 28 August 1960 letter + excerpt from *Middle
    East Diary*, and unsigned typed comment.

1 - 27 October 1960 - tls; "as from Sury" [Saintes];
    Professor Miriam J. Benkovitz, c/o Skidmore
    College, Saratoga Springs, New York.

Harald, Mrs. Michael; 1 letter

    1 - 24 January 1961 - tls; Aix-en-Provence; Professor
        Miriam J. Benkovitz, c/o Skidmore College, Saratoga
        Springs, New York.

Harding-Edgar, B. (English rare-book dealer who moved to
                Spain); 1 letter

    1 - 5 November 1948 - tls, Le Lavandou, SUNY.

Harrison, Michael (editor, writer); 4 letters

    1 - 2 March 1956 - tls, Montpellier, UT, + two
        leaflets regarding Algerian situation.

    2 - 14 November 1957 and 24 January 1958 - tls, Sury,
        UT.

    1 - 21 February 1962 - tls, Aix-en-Provence, UT.

Hatch, Mr. (Viking Press, Inc.); 1 letter

    1 - 13 February 1940 - tls, New York City, V.

William Heinemann, Ltd. (publishers); 1 letter

    1 - 17 December 1955 - tls, Montpellier, H.

Holroyd-Reece, John (journalist, translator; publisher
                of reprints of several of Aldington's
                books in Albatross Editions); 5
                letters

    1 - 18 December 1952 - telegram (copy), n.p., UT.

    2 - 18 December 1952 and 5 May 1953 - tls, Montpellier,
        UT.

    1 - 28 December 1952 - tl, Montpellier, SIU, + two
        pages "Replies to Quiries" and two pages "Notes
        on Joynson-Hicks Memorandum."

    1 - 30 September 1954 - tls, Montpellier, SIU, +
        copy.

Horne and Birkett (Aldington's attorneys); 1 letter

    1 - 7 January 1957 - tl, Westminister, SIU.

Huebsch, Benjamin W. (American publisher; translator,
                music critic, editor); 2 letters

    2 - 4 May and 12 June 1950 - tls, Le Lavandou, LC.

Hughes, Babette (novelist; wife of Glenn Hughes);

                4 letters

    1 - 23 January 1928 - tls, Padworth, UT.

    1 - 1 June 1928 - tli, "Written in Paris," UT.

    1 - 7 February 1929 - apcs; Portofino, Italy; UT.

    1 - 22 May 1929 - tls, Paris, UT.

Hughes, Babette and Glenn; 6 letters

    1 - 31 August 1928 - tls, Padworth, UT.

    1 - 14 March 1929 - tls, Select, UT.

    1 - 16 May 1929 - als, Select, UT.

    2 - 4 and 7 August 1929 - tls; c/o Barclays Bank,

        Paris; UT.

    1 - n.d. - tls, Select, UT.

Hughes, Glenn A. (poet, playwright, professor of drama,

                editor, critic); 46 letters

    1 - n.d. - ans, n.p., UT.

  11 - 1 August 1925 to 29 November 1927 - tls, Padworth,

      UT.

    9 - 16 February 1926 to 28 July 1928 - tli, Padworth,

      UT.

    1 - 10 April 1927 - ali; c/o Barclays Bank, Paris;

      UT.

    1 - 12 August 1927 - ali, Padworth, UT.

    2 - 14 and 22 September 1928 - tli, Rome, UT.

    2 - 20 and 28 September 1928 - apci, Rome, UT.

    3 - 10 and 16 October, 9 November 1928 - tli;

      La Vigie, Ile de Port-Cros, Var; UT.

    2 - 15 and 26 October 1928 - ali; La Vigie, Ile de

      Port-Cros, Var; UT.

    3 - 10 December 1928, 1 March and 16 May 1929 - tli,

      Select, UT.

    2 - 2 and 14 January 1929 - tli, Rapallo, UT.

    1 - 14 March 1929 - tls, Select, UT.

1 - n.d. [2 April 1929] - apcs, Paris, UT.

1 - 12 June 1929 - telegram, Paris, UT.

4 - 16 October 1929 to 27 November 1930 - tls; c/o
    Barclays Bank, Paris; UT.

1 - 18 November 1929 - tli, Rome, UT.

1 - 7 December 1929 - tli; Amalfi, Italy; UT.

Hunt, Violet (novelist and short-story writer; second
            wife of Ford Madox Ford); 1 letter

1 - 9 November 1921 - als, Authors' Club, NYPL.

Hutchens, Patricia (wife of Richard Graesen; author of
            books on Pound and Joyce); 4 letters

2 - 1 and 31 October 1953 - tls, Montpellier, SIU.

2 - 9 January 1958 and 19 October 1959 - tls, Sury,
    SIU.

Hynes, S. L. (professor of English, Northwestern University;
            author and editor); 2 letters

2 - 30 April and 15 May 1954 - tls, Montpellier, UT.

Isaac, Elizabeth (University of Washington Bookstore);
            1 letter

1 - 22 September 1927 - als, Padworth, UW.

Jackson, Holbrook (writer, editor, publisher); 11 letters

10 - 25 June 1921 to 2 April [?] 1923 - als, Padworth,
     SUNY.

1 - 18 December 1922 - tls, Padworth, SUNY.

Johnson, Martyn (editor of *Dial*, New York); 4 letters

1 - n.d. [1917-1918] - als, Mecklenburg Square, UT.

2 - 29 July and 4 August 1917 - als, Mecklenburg
    Square, UT.

1 - 17 February 1919 - als, Rye, UT.

Jonas, Klaus, W. (Professor, Rutgers University; editor);
            2 letters

2 - 21 December 1950 and 5 February 1951 - tls, Le
    Lavandou, UT.

Jones, Zuleika (fictitious name coined by Aldington's
               friends); 1 letter

    1 - 1 August 1929 - tls; c/o Barclays Bank, Paris; HU.
Joyce, James (Irish poet, short-story writer and novelist);
               3 letters

    1 - 6 May 1919 - als, Authors' Club, CU.

    1 - 10 March 1927 - tls, Padworth, SUNY.

    1 - 12 December 1928 - tls, Select, SUNY.
Joynson-Hicks & Co. (solicitors who acted for Aldington
                    and Collins in clearing publication
                    of book on T. E. Lawrence); 1 letter

    1 - 25 October 1955 - tl, London, SIU.
Kershaw, Alister (Aldington's literary executor; onetime
                  secretary and devoted admirer and friend);
                  1201 letters

    7 - 14 May to 24 July 1947 - tls, Montparnasse, SIU.

  226 - 6 August 1947 to 25 April 1951 - tls, Le Lavandou,
        SIU, letters 29 January 1949 + carbon copy same
        date to Wreden, 2 March 1949 + copy annotated
        letter to *TLS*, 11 March 1951 + extracts from a
        letter of 14 April 1927 from T. E. Shaw to Mrs.
        G. B. Shaw.

    2 - 31 October and 1 November 1950 - apci, Le
        Lavandou, SIU.

    1 - 21 November 1950 - als, n.p., SIU.

    2 - 3 and 11 April 1951 - als, Le Lavandou, SIU.

    1 - 28 April 1951 - apci, Avignon, SIU.

    1 - 4 May 1951 - als, Montpellier, SIU.

    4 - 25 May 1951 to 14 November 1951 - apcs,
        Montpellier, SIU.

    1 - 6 May 1951 - apcs, Carcassone, SIU.

    1 - 7 May 1951 - als, Carcassone, SIU.

    1 - 12 May 1951 - tls, Saint-Gemme, SIU.

1 - 17 May 1951 - als, Aveynon, SIU.

1 - 18 May 1951 - apcs; Albi, Hérault; SIU.

580 - 19 May 1951 to 23 July 1959 - tls, Montpellier,
     SIU, letter 21 May 1954 + carbon of 29 March 1954
     letter from Freida Lawrence, and tls of 18 May
     1954 from Graham Green.

1 - 24 May 1951 - apcs; Aigues-Mortes, Gard; SIU.

1 - 25 May 1951 - apcs; Saint-Guilhem-le-Desert,
    (Hérault); SIU.

4 - 25 May 1951 to 14 November 1951 - apcs,
    Montpellier, SIU.

3 - 31 May 1951 [*sic*, all same date] - apcs, Arles, SIU.

1 - 14 June 1951 - apcs, Environs de Ganges, SIU.

2 - 30 August and 3 October 1951 - apci, Montpellier,
    SIU.

1 - 15 November 1951 - apcs, Pierre-Buffiere, SIU.

6 - 5 to 17 July 1952 - tls; La Falaise, St. Clair,
    Le Lavandou; SIU.

1 - 27 March 1953 - apcs, Vaucluse, SIU.

1 - 31 March 1953 - als; À Daou, St. Clair, par Le
    Lavandou, Var; SIU.

1 - 16 April 1954 - tls; À Daou, St. Clair, par Le
    Lavandou, Var; SIU.

2 - 17 June 1954 and 5 April 1955 - apcs, Saintes,
    SIU.

1 - 22 December 1954 - apcs, Genoa, SIU.

1 - 25 July 1957 - apcs, Riom, SIU.

1 - 29 July 1957 - apcs, Sancerre, SIU.

1 - 8 August 1957 - tls, Sancerre, SIU.

3 - 10, 11 and 12 August 1957 - tls; Hotel Point du
    Jour, Sancerre; SIU.

263 - 19 August 1957 to 18 July 1962 - tls, Sury, SIU.

1 - 1 January 1959 - apcs, Monaco, SIU.

1 - 2 January 1959 - apcs, Cannes, SIU.

1 - 2 January 1959 - apcs; À Daou, St. Clair, par Le
    Lavandou, Var; SIU.

1 - 24 November 1959 - apcs, Zurich, SIU.

5 - 4 June 1960 to 25 September 1961 - tls, Saintes,
    SIU.

3 - 28 June and 1 July 1960, 10 May 1962 - apcs,
    Saintes, SIU.

47 - 14 October 1960 to 22 February 1962 - tls, Aix-
    en-Provence, SIU.

2 - 28 February and 27 May 1961 - apcs, Sury, SIU.

1 - 14 March 1961 - apcs; Orange, Vaucluse; SIU.

2 - 22 March and 22 November 1961 - apcs, Aix-en-
    Provence, SIU.

9 - 15 April to 20 May 1961 - apcs, Venice, SIU.

1 - 24 April 1961 - als, Venice, SIU.

1 - 15 May 1961 - als, "Mas Dromar" [written from
    Venice], SIU.

1 - 23 September 1961 - als, "En Camargue," SIU.

1 - 22 June 1962 - apcs, Paris, SIU.

1 - 25 June 1962 - apcs, Moscow, SIU.

1 - 28 June 1962 - als, n.p. [Leningrad], SIU.

1 - 30 June 1962 - apcs, Leningrad, SIU.

1 - "Sunday" - tls, Montpellier, SIU.

1 - n.d. - tls, n.p., SIU.

Kershaw, Shelia (second wife of Alister; once with UNESCO);
                1 letter

1 - 9 April 1962 - tls, Sury, SIU.

Knollenberg, Bernard (librarian, Sterling Library, Yale
                University); 5 letters

1 - 15 June 1940 - tls, Old Lyme, YU.

1 - 17 December 1940 - als, Washington, YU.

3 - 15 and 26 May, 27 June 1942 - tls, Jamay, YU.

Kreymbourg, Alfred (American poet, playwright, critic, and
                chessmaster); 1 letter

   1 - [c. 1921] - tl copy, n.p., UT.

Langham, Dr. S. T. (an M.D., in 1952 lieutenant in the
                Royal Army Medical Corps who enjoyed
                Aldington's autobiography); 2 letters

   2 - 21 June 1952 and 2 October 1955 - tls; Montpellier;
    Professor Miriam J. Benkovitz, c/o Skidmore
    College, Saratoga Springs, New York.

Laughlin, Mr. (James Laughlin, founder of New Directions
                Publishing?); 1 letter

   1 - 26 January 1951 - tl, Le Lavandou, SIU.

Lawrence, Frieda (wife of D. H. Lawrence [her second
                husband] and later Mrs. Angelo Ravagli);
                16 letters

   3 - 19 December 1940, 16 January and 1 February 1941
    - tls, Washington, UT.

   5 - 20 March to 31 December 1941 - tls, Jamay, UT.

   1 - 27 September 1941 - als; Marianna, Florida; UT.

   7 - 29 May 1954 to 7 February 1956 - tls, Montpellier,
    UT.

Lawrence, Professor (A. W. Lawrence, brother of T. E.
                Lawrence); 1 letter

   1 - 30 June 1950 - tls, Le Lavandou, SIU.

Layton, Mr.; 1 letter

   1 - 27 February 1954 - tls, Montpellier, SIU.

Lehmann, John (publisher, poet, man of letters, literary
                promoter-entrepreneur); 2 letters

   2 - 19 May and 11 June 1955 - tls, Montpellier, UT.

Lewis, Percy Wyndham (English satirist, painter, leader
                of Vorticism); 23 letters

   1 - n.d. - als; Hindhead, Surry; CU.

   1 - "13 December" - tls, London, CU (on letterhead

of *The Egoist*).

1 - "St. George's Day" - tli, London, CU.

2 - 25 and 28 July 1928 - tls, Padworth, CU.

1 - 18 September 1928 - als, Rome, CU.

3 - 17 and 28 September 1929, 17 September 1930 -
tls, Paris, CU.

1 - 8 October 1929 - telegram copy, Paris, CU.

2 - 17 and 28 October 1929 - tli, Paris, CU.

1 - 22 November 1929 - tli, Rome, CU.

2 - 7 October 1932 and 11 December 1933 - als, London,
CU.

1 - 20 October 1932 - als, Lisbon, CU.

3 - 16 December 1933, 13 February and 29 March 1934
- tls, London, CU.

1 - 22 April 1934 - tli, London, CU.

1 - n.d. [1935 or 1936] - tli, n.p. [London], CU.

1 - 26 March 1935 - tls, Tobago, CU.

1 - 12 October 1936 - tls, n.p. [London], CU.

Loving, Edward Pierre (writer and editor; staff *New York*
Herald, Paris, 1925; advising editor
This Quarter, Paris, 1929); 1 letter

1 - 16 June 1929 - tls; c/o Barclays Bank, Paris; UT.

Lowell, Amy (American poet, critic, essayist, patron of
artists; took over Imagist anthologies after
first); 102 letters

15 - 11 May 1914 to 8 January 1916 - als, Hampstead, HU.

1 - "Wednesday night" [30 July 1914] - apcs, n.p.
[London], HU.

1 - 21 September 1914 - photocopy of als, Kensington,
UT.

3 - 21 September, 8 October and 30 December 1914 -
als, Kensington, HU.

6 - 3 October to 7 December 1914 - tls, Kensington,

HU.

3 - 6 November and 14 December 1914, 4 April 1917 -
   als, n.p., HU.

1 - 4 December 1914 - als, "British Museum," HU.

3 - 5 December 1914 to 11 April 1915 - tls,
   Bloomsbury, HU.

2 - 7 December 1914 to 6 May 1915 - apci, Bloomsbury,
   HU.

7 - 26 December 1914 to 8 December 1916 - als,
   Bloomsbury, HU.

10 - 22 February 1915 to 3 February 1916 - tls,
    Hampstead, HU.

2 - n.d. [1 March] and 1 October 1915 - apci,
   Hampstead, HU.

1 - 22 April 1915 - apcs, Bloomsbury, HU.

3 - 27 March to 22 June 1916 - als, Woodland Cottage,
   HU.

1 - 11 June 1916 - tls, Woodland Cottage, HU.

1 - 30 June 1916 - als; BEF (Wareham, Dorset); HU.

1 - 1 October 1916 - als, BEF ("c/o H.D."), HU.

3 - 4 January 1917 to 8 December 1918 - als, BEF
   (France), HU.

1 - 20 November 1917 - photocopy of als, n.p., UT.

1 - 20 November 1917 - als, n.p. [Officers' Training
   Camp], HU.

4 - 2 January to 12 April 1918 - als, Mecklenburg
   Square, HU.

3 - 8 December 1918, [January ?] and 21 February 1919
   - als, Rye, HU.

10 - 27 February 1919 to 16 November 1920 - als,
    Authors' Club, HU.

5 - 5 January to 14 May 1920 - als, Hermitage, HU.

3 - 17 June to 12 October 1920 - tls, Hermitage, HU.

4 - 7 April 1921 to 5 May 1922 - als, Padworth, HU.

6 - 1 April 1922 to 2 March 1925 - tls, Padworth, HU.

1 - 4 May 1925 - apci, Shrewsbury, HU.

Lyle, Rob (English poet; wrote on Mistral; participated
          in preparing unpublished attack on critics of
          Pinorman); 102 letters

99 - 20 July 1954 to 19 October 1956 - tls, Montpellier,
          NYPL.

3 - 12 March, 7 and 8 April 1955 - telegrams,
          Montpellier, NYPL.

Machin, Mr.; 1 letter

1 - 1 June 1961 - tl, Sury, enclosed with letter to
          Harry T. Moore.

Mackie, Mrs. (connected with Lawrence ranch in New Mexico);
          1 letter

1 - 22 February 1941 - tls, Washington, UT.

MacLeish, Archibald (American poet, verse dramatist,
          essayist); 2 letters

2 - 12 and 27 February 1941 - tls, Washington, LC.

Malcolm, [?]; 1 letter

1 - 28 August 1935 - tls, Old Lyme, SIU.

Manning, Frederic (Australian born; lived in England; poet,
          writer); 2 letters

1 - 19 October 1920 - als, Hermitage, UCLA.

1 - 12 March 1921 - als, Padworth, UCLA.

Manuel, Alvin George (Aldington's Hollywood agent); 141
          letters

1 - 19 April 1940 - tls; c/o Viking Press, New York
          City; UCLA.

3 - 29 April to 13 May 1940 - tls, New York City, UCLA.

2 - 6 and 10 July 1940 - tls, Old Lyme, UCLA.

7 - 23 April to 26 August 1942 - tls, Jamay, UCLA.

1 - 26 June 1942 - tl, Jamay, UCLA.

 2 - 26 and 29 July 1942 - tls; Boulder, Colorado; UCLA.

 1 - 7 September 1942 - als; Boulder, Colorado; UCLA.

12 - 30 September 1942 to 1 November 1945 - tls,
     Hollywood, UCLA.

 1 - 7 July 1943 - tl draft and copy, Hollywood, UCLA.

 1 - n.d. [1943] - tls, n.p., UCLA.

 1 - 8 April 1944 - tls, n.p., UCLA.

 1 - 9 June 1944 - tls; "The Can," Burbank, California;
     UCLA.

 3 - 18, 19 and 26 May 1946 - als, Jamaica, UCLA.

 7 - 4 June to 29 July 1946 - tls, Jamaica, UCLA.

 1 - 14 July 194[6, reads "1945" in error] - tls,
     Jamaica, UCLA.

 1 - 4 August 1946 - als; Hotel Commodore, New York
     City; UCLA.

 2 - 5 and 8 August 1946 - tls; Hotel Commodore, New
     York City; UCLA, + tl copy of the 5 August letter.

 1 - 11 August 1946 - telegram; Drake Hotel, New York
     City; UCLA.

10 - 3 September to 13 December 1946 - tls; c/o
     American Express, Paris, UCLA.

 1 - 8 January 1947 - tl, Montparnasse, UCLA.

11 - 20 January to 12 June 1947 - tls, Montparnasse,
     UCLA.

 1 - 22 July 1947 - tls; Chez Agence Lugon, Le
     Lavandou; UCLA.

56 - 6 August 1947 to 24 April 1951 - tls, Le
     Lavandou, UCLA.

 2 - 23 January and 18 March 1948 - telegram, Le
     Lavandou, UCLA.

 1 - 17 November 1948 - tl, Le Lavandou, UCLA.

11 - 30 June 1951 to 12 November 1956 - tls, Montpellier,
     UCLA.

Marshall, Kenneth W.; 4 letters
    4 - 16 September to 2 October 1929 - tls, Corneille,
      NYPL.

Mathews, Elkin (publisher); 2 letters
    1 - n.d. [1919?] - als, n.p. [London], YU.
    1 - 7 June 1919 - als, Authors' Club, TU.

May, Mr. (editor?); 2 letters
    2 - 29 April and 23 May 1919 - als, Authors' Club, YU,
      + ms "A Roman Letter."

Megata, Morikimi (professor of English at Kobe City
                University of Foreign Studies; admirer
                of Aldington; published letters of
                Aldington in Japan; critic and essayist);
                34 letters
    1 - n.d. [between 1952 and 1962] - apci, n.p.
      [Montpellier or Sury], recipient.
    1 - n.d. [between 1952 and 1962] - apcs, n.p.
      [Montpellier or Sury], recipient.
   14 - 25 May 1952 to 29 August 1956 - tls, Montpellier,
      recipient. Published in *Kobe City University*
      Journal, October 1969, January 1970, July 1970 and
      July 1971.
   17 - 5 March 1958 to 24 April 1962 - tls, Sury,
      recipient. Published in *Kobe City University*
      Journal, October 1969, January 1970, July 1970
      and July 1971.
    1 - 18 November 1961 - apcs "Richard and Catherine
      Aldington," Aix-en-Provence, recipient.

Metcalf, John and James Southall Wilson (editors of *The*
                Enchanted Years); 1 letter
    1 - 19 January 1921 - als, Padworth, UV.

Miller, D. (vice-consul, British Consulate General,
                Marseille); 1 letter

1 - 27 January 1948 - tl copy, Le Lavandou, SIU.

Miner, Earl Roy (professor of English, Princeton University; interpreter; scholar of Japanese literature, essayist, editor, author); 3 letters

3 - 30 January, 24 February and 4 April 1951 - tls, Le Lavandou, UCLA.

Monro, Harold (poet, anthologist, editor; operated Poetry Bookshop; issued Chapbooks; edited *Poetry Review* and *Poetry and Drama*); 125 letters

4 - n.d. - als, n.p., UCLA.

1 - n.d. - als; 12 Rue de la Franche (?), Chaumière, Paris; UCLA.

1 - n.d. - als, Hermitage, UCLA.

3 - [1911] - als, Twickenham, UCLA.

1 - 19 December 1911 - als, Twickenham, UCLA.

2 - 25 May and 22 October 1914 - tls, Kensington, UCLA.

1 - July [?] - 1914 - als, n.p., UCLA.

1 - n.d. - apcs, Kensington, UCLA.

2 - 5 November 1914 and 20 January 1915 - als, Kensington, UCLA.

3 - n.d. [1914] - tls, Kensington, UCLA.

1 - n.d. [1914] - als, Kensington, UCLA.

1 - 14 [January or July ?] 1915 - als, Bloomsbury, UCLA.

5 - 22 February 1915 to 18 February 1916 - tls, Hampstead, UCLA.

5 - n.d. [30 March] to 12 November 1915 - als, Hampstead, UCLA.

2 - 22 April and 7 May 1915 - apcs, Hampstead, UCLA.

1 - n.d. [1915] - als, Hampstead, UCLA.

2 - 18 June 1916 and 6 December 1920 - als, Woodland Cottage, UCLA.

4 - n.d. [1916] - als, Hampstead, UCLA.

1 - n.d. [1916] - tls, Hampstead, UCLA.

1 - n.d. [1916] - als; c/o Mrs. Delbridge, Paracombe,
    N. Devons.; UCLA.

1 - 31 March 1919 - als, Littoral, UCLA.

9 - 23 March to 10 November 1920 - als, Hermitage,
    UCLA.

6 - 8 June to 28 September 1920 - tls, Hermitage,
    UCLA.

32 - 12 January 1921 to 9 July 1927 - als, Padworth,
     UCLA.

2 - 26 October 1921 and 6 July 1922 - apcs, n.p.,
    UCLA.

22 - 8 December 1921 to 9 July 1927 - tls, Padworth,
     UCLA.

1 - 29 March 1922 - tls, Padworth, UVI. Published by
    Professor David S. Thatcher with Read letters in
    "Richard Aldington's Letters to Herbert Read,"
    The Malahat Review, 15 (July 1970), 5-44.

1 - 31 March 1922 - tls, Padworth, UVI.

1 - 15 June 1922 - als; Sherryford, Paracombe, N.
    Devons.; UCLA.

1 - 1 January 1924 - als, Rome, UCLA.

1 - 18 August 1925 - als, Padworth, UT.

2 - n.d. [1925] - als, n.p., UCLA.

1 - 30 March 1928 - als; c/o Barclays Bank, Paris;
    UCLA.

1 - 28 December 1928 - tls; c/o Barclays Bank, Paris;
    UCLA.

1 - 15 June 1929 - tls; c/o Barclays Bank, Paris;
    SUNY, + carbon tls from Monro.

1 - 4 August 1929 - tls; Hotel Rivage de Fabrégas,
    Fabrégas, La Seyne, Var; SUNY, + carbon tls from
    Monro.

Monroe, Harriet (founder and first editor of *Poetry: A Magazine of Verse*); 79 letters

   1 - 26 November 1912 - als, n.p., UC.

   1 - 5 July 1913 - als, Paris, UC.

  24 - 6 October 1913 to 28 November 1920 - als, London, UC.

   1 - n.d. [1914] - ans, n.p., UC.

  13 - 17 March 1914 to 8 July 1915 - tls, London, UC.

   1 - 15 March 1915 - ans, London, UC.

   1 - 1 October 1915 - tls, Hampstead, UC.

   1 - 29 November 1915 - als, Hampstead, UC.

   1 - 8 December 1918 - als, n.p., UC.

   2 - 24 December 1918 and 17 February 1919 - als, Rye, UC.

   9 - 10 December 1919 to 3 November 1920 - als, Hermitage, UC.

   7 - 15 April to 13 November 1920 - tls, Hermitage, UC.

  13 - 15 December 1920 to n.d. [1924] - als, Padworth, UC.

   2 - 9 January 1922 and 22 September 1924 - tls, Padworth, UC.

   2 - n.d. - als, n.p., UC.

de Montalk, Count Geoffrey (pretender to the throne of Poland; writer, scholar, private printer and poet); 97 letters

   2 - 26 January and 26 March 1930 - tls and typed copies of each; c/o Barclays Bank, Paris, SIU.

  39 - 29 September 1954 to 28 June 1957 - tls, Montpellier, SIU, 28 April 1955 + copy tls J. F. Breen to Aldington; 9 June 1955 + news clipping; 25 June 1955 + signed statement re: Sir Ernest Wild; 19 August 1955 + news clipping; 28 June 1956

+ tls Mark Bonham-Carter to Aldington; 2 December
1956 + tls Wladyslaw to Joan Armitage 13 November
1956; 7 May and 3 June 1957 + newspaper clippings.

51 - 2 October 1957 to 22 July 1961 - tls, Sury, SIU,
26 December 1957 + poem (not Aldington's); 26
April 1959 + printed page re: Frederic Mistral;
4 May 1959 + typed note re: Naval Research; 3
February 1960 + French poem by Catherine
Aldington; 22 July 1961 + newspaper clipping.

1 - 14 February 1959 - telegram, Sury, SIU.

4 - 4 December 1960 to 28 November 1961 - tls,
Aix-en-Provence, SIU.

Moore, Harry T. (professor of English, Southern Illinois
University; scholar, biographer, essayist,
editor); 56 letters

39 - 23 October 1958 to 9 June 1962 - tls Sury,
recipient, 12 April 1962 + newspaper clipping;
28 February 1961 + tls Cyril Upton to Aldington
dated 23 February 1961.

1 - 29 June 1959 - tls copy; Poste Restante,
Montpellier, Hérault; recipient.

1 - 29 April 1961 - als; "As from Sury en Vaux, Cher"
[Venice]; recipient.

14 - 14 October 1961 to 16 February 1962 - tls,
Aix-en-Provence, recipient, 22 November 1961
+ newspaper clipping.

1 - [between 10 and 27 July 1962] - tls, Sury,
recipient. (Professor Moore was unable to locate
this letter, but is sure of its existence.)

Moore, Marianne (American poet)

It is possible that there are a few letters in the
Marianne Moore Collection at the Rosenbach Museum,
Philadelphia, Pa.

Moore, Thomas Sturge (poet, aesthetic theorist, art
                        historian, graphic artist [book
                        designer]); 10 letters
    1 - 30 March 1918 - als, BEF (Tunbridge Wells), UL.
    1 - 28 December 1919 - als, Hermitage, IU.
    1 - 14 November 1920 - als, Hermitage, UL.
    1 - 11 December 1920 - als, Woodland Cottage, UL.
    4 - 7 April 1921 to 11 January 1922 - als, Padworth,
        IU.
    2 - 19 and 25 January 1922 - tls, Padworth, IU.
Morrell, Lady Ottoline (aristocratic patron of the arts,
                        eccentric); 4 letters
    1 - 18 July 1922 - tls, Padworth, UT.
    3 - 25 July, 3 and 27 August 1922 - als, Padworth, UT.
Morris, Guido (book dealer); 1 letter
    1 - 1953 - tls, n.p.; G. F. Sims, Hurst, Reading,
        Berkshire; listed in his Catalogue 84.
Moult, Thomas (poet, critic, editor, novelist,
                        anthologist); 4 letters
    1 - 21 June 1920 - als, Hermitage, NYPL.
    1 - 20 July 1920 - tls, Hermitage, NYPL.
    1 - 26 January 1923 - tls, Padworth, NYPL.
    1 - 26 July 1935 - tls, Old Lyme, NYPL.
Munson, Mr.; 1 letter
    1 - 23 January 1936 - tls, London, SIU.
Murry, J. Middleton (critic, journalist, biographer;
                        edited *Adelphi*); 1 letter
    1 - 2 May 1950 - tls, Le Lavandou, UT.
Nehls, Edward (professor, University of Wisconsin;
                        compiled *D. H. Lawrence: A Composite
                        Biography* to which Aldington contributed);
                        29 letters
    13 - 18 January 1952 to 16 August 1956 - tls,

Montpellier, UT.

 16 - 24 August 1957 to 24 January 1959 - tls, Sury,
  UT.

Nethercot, Arthur Hobart (professor, Northwestern
       University; critic, essayist,
       author); 2 letters

 1 - 15 February 1922 - tls, Padworth, SIU.

 1 - 17 January 1924 - tls, Rome, SIU.

Noble, Barbara (Doubleday and Co., Inc.); 1 letter

 1 - 23 July 1956 - tls, Montpellier, H.

Norman, Charles (American biographer of Ezra Pound and
      others); 7 letters

 1 - 19 February 1959 - tls, Sury, UT.

 6 - 5 November 1960 to 17 May 1962 - tls, Sury, UT.

Orioli, Guiseppe ("Pino") (publisher, editor, Florentine
       bookseller, writer; companion
       of Norman Douglas); 22 letters

 1 - 25 March 1931 - apcs, Rome, UT.

 1 - 26 September 1933 - apcs; Condom, Gascony; SIU.

 1 - 9 May 1934 - als; Amarante, Portugal; UT.

 1 - 10 April 1935 - tls, Tobago, UT.

 1 - 20 March 1936 - tls; Cavendish Hotel, Jerymn St.,
  London; UT.

 1 - 11 January 1937 - apcs; Portofino, Italy; SIU.

 1 - 24 January 1937 - apcs, Brantôme, SIU.

 1 - 26 January 1937 - als, Bordeaux, SIU.

 1 - 3 February 1937 - tls, Toulon, SIU.

 1 - 3 March 1937 - als, Capri, UT.

 1 - 10 March 1937 - tls; Hotel Suisse, Marin Grande,
  Capri; SIU.

 7 - 9 May 1937 to 1 January 1939 - tls, Le Canadel,
  SIU.

 3 - 17 July 1937, 9 February and 12 December 1938 -

tls, Le Canadel, UT.

1 - n.d. - als, n.p., SIU.

Palmer, Herbert E. (poet and literary journalist); 1 letter

1 - 16 March 1938 - tls, Le Canadel, UT.

Parker, Robert Allerton (American biographer; writer on

popular religious movements);

9 letters

4 - 10 August to 2 November 1956 - tls, Montpellier,
UCB

5 - 3 September 1957 to 28 July 1960 - tls, Sury, UCB.

Patmore, Brigit (wife of Deighton Patmore, grandson of

Coventry Patmore; writer, translator,

Aldington's long-time mistress); 158

letters

1 - 4 December 1928 - als, "Paris," UT.

25 - 12 December 1928 to 2 April 1930 - telegrams,
Paris, UT.

1 - 15 December 1928 - als; Chope Latine, Boulevard
St. Michael; UT.

1 - 23 December 1928 - als, Authors' Club, UT, +
als to Manager, Barclays Bank, Reading, Berkshire.

1 - 25 December 1928 - telegram, Isle of Thanet, UT.

1 - n.d. [4 May 1929] - apc, n.p. [Paris], UT.

1 - 11 May 1929 - tls, Select, UT.

3 - 14, 15, and 16 May 1929 - als, Select, UT.

2 - 30 March 1930 - als; Resturante Voltaire, 1,
Place de l'Odéon, Paris; UT.

1 - 7 April 1930 - telegram, London, UT.

1 - 5 February 1931 - als, "Bretagna," UT.

3 - 6 and 8 February 1931, 18 September 1932 - als,
n.p., UT.

6 - 8 to 15 February 1931 - als, Florence, UT.

2 - 8 and 25 February 1931 - telegram, Florence, UT.

1 - 12 September 1932 - als; Brantôme, Dordogne,
    France; UT.

8 - 12 to 19 September 1932 - apcs; Brantôme,
    Dordogne, France; UT.

1 - 19 September 1932 - telegram; Brantôme, Dordogne,
    France; UT.

1 - 20 September 1932 - tls; Brantôme, Dordogne,
    France; UT.

1 - n.d. [30 September 1932] - apci; 26 Porchester
    Square, [London]; UT.

1 - 28 January 1933 - tls; Christ Church, Oxford; UT.

1 - n.d. [between June and September 1934] - tls;
    Alpenhotel, Fernpass in Tirol, Austria; UT.

1 - 2 November 1937 - tls; Stanmer, Lewes, Sussex; UT.

1 - "Tuesday" - al (last page[s] missing), n.p., UT.

1 - "Thursday" - als, "Paris," UT.

1 - "Thur" - als, "in train," UT.

1 - "Thursday evening" - als; Chapelle-Reanville,
    Eure, France; UT.

2 - n.d. - als, Authors' Club, UT.

11 - n.d. - als; Chope Latine, Boulevard St. Michael;
    UT.

2 - n.d. - als; Resturante Voltaire, 1, Place de
    l'Odéon, Paris; UT.

28 - n.d. - als, Select, UT.

2 - n.d. - tls, Select, UT.

5 - n.d. - als, "Paris," UT.

31 - n.d. - als, n.p., UT.

2 - n.d. - al (first four pages missing), n.p., UT.

1 - n.d. - ans, n.p., UT.

2 - n.d. - ani, n.p., UT.

3 - n.d. - an, n.p., UT.

1 - n.d. - an (fragment), n.p., UT.

Patmore, Derek (writer, essayist, coauthor of play with
              Aldington; son of Brigit Patmore,
              brother-in-law of Aldington's second wife);
              47 letters

2 - 6 and 24 March 1928 - tls, Padworth, SIU.

1 - 14 May 1928 - tls, "Written from Paris," SIU.

1 - n.d. [ca. January 1929] - tls, n.p., SIU.

1 - 6 February 1929 - tls, Rapallo, SIU.

1 - 16 February 1929 - telegram, Paris, SIU.

2 - "Tuesday," "Sunday" [ca. March 1929] - tls,
    Select, SIU.

8 - 24 September to 19 October 1929 - tls,
    Corneille, SIU.

1 - 4 December 1929 - tls, Sorrento, SIU.

2 - 10 and [?] December 1929 - tls, Amalfi, SIU.

1 - 24 December 1929 - tls, Palermo, SIU.

5 - 11 to 26 January 1930 - tls, Tunis, SIU.

4 - 30 April to 26 June 1930 - tls, Ursulines, SIU.

1 - 9 August 1930 - tls; Villa le Bouquet,
    Aiguebelle, par Le Lavandou, Var; SIU.

2 - 29 September and 25 October 1930 - tls, Venice,
    SIU.

5 - 10 December 1930 to 10 April 1932 - tls,
    Florence, SIU.

1 - 29 April 1931 - als, *Lyris* ("just off Marseilles"),
    SIU.

1 - 10 July 1931 - tls, Le Canadel, SIU.

1 - 25 January 1932 - tli, Florence, UT.

1 - 9 December 1932 - tls, Lisbon, UT.

1 - 16 December 1932 - apcs, Bordeaux, UT.

2 - 15 June and 30 August 1933 - tls, Pramousquier,
    SIU.

1 - 9 February 1935 - als, [S.S.] *Ariguara*, UT.

1 - 22 April 1935 - tls, Tobago, UT.

1 - 11 July 1936 - tls; Fernpass in Tirol, Austria;
UT.

[Pearce?], Charles; 1 letter

1 - 13 June 1950 - tl, Le Lavandou, SIU.

Pearson, Norman Holmes (Yale professor of English and
American literature; literary
scholar, editor, was literary
executor for H. D. who was
Aldington's first wife); 3 letters

1 - 21 February 1937 - tls, c/o Heinemann, YU-P.

2 - 27 July and 29 August 1961 - tls, Sury, YU-P.

Pinker, James B. and Sons (literary agents who represented
Aldington); 11 letters

9 - 28 May 1939 to 5 January 1940 - tls; c/o Viking
Press, 18 E. 48th St., New York City; NYPL.

1 - 6 June 1939 - tls; Crowfield, Saundersfield, R.I.;
NYPL.

1 - n.d. - tls; c/o Viking Press, 18 E. 48th St.,
New York City; NYPL.

Pinker, J. Ralph (literary agent, convicted of misuse of
clients' funds; Aldington's agent); 195
letters

10 - 5 February 1929 to 25 March 1930 - tls; c/o
Barclays Bank, Paris; SIU, + newspaper clipping
with 19 March 1930.

10 - 22 September to 1 November 1929 - tls, Corneille,
SIU.

2 - 14 and 15 November 1929 - tls, Rome, SIU.

7 - 18 November to 8 December 1929 - tls, Naples, SIU.

9 - 10 December to 30 December 1929 - tls, Palermo,
SIU.

1 - 24 December 1929 - telegram, Palermo, SIU.

10 - 3 January to 3 February 1930 - tls, Tunis, SIU.

2 - 5 and 17 February 1930 - tls, Algiers, SIU, 5
February + newspaper clipping 7 February 1930
Evening World, Bristol.

1 - 12 February 1930 - apcs; Touggourt, Algeria; SIU.

1 - 16 March 1930 - als, Paris, SIU.

1 - 12 April 1930 - tls, "Garlands Hotel," SIU.

3 - 18 (2), and 24 April 1930 - tls, Ursulines, SIU,
+ telegram 18 April letter, + records of
Aldington's account from Covici, Freide, Inc.
with 24 April letter.

1 - 22 September 1930 - tls; Le Bouquet, Aiguebelle,
par Le Lavandou, Var; SIU.

4 - 27 September to [?] November 1930 - tls;
c/o Barclays Bank, Paris; SIU.

1 - 29 September 1930 - tls, n.p. [Paris], SIU.

10 - 7 October to 13 November 1930 - tls, Venice,
SIU.

3 - 15, 18 and 23 November 1930 - tls, Brindisi, SIU,
18 November + newspaper clipping.

1 - 2 May 1931 - tls, Le Lavandou, SIU.

1 - 2 May 1931 - als, Le Lavandou, SIU.

23 - 5 May to 19 July 1931 - tls, Le Canadel, SIU,
12 July + tls from C. B. Purdo dated 9 July
1931, London.

1 - 5 May 1931 - apcs, Marseille, SIU.

1 - 27 July 1931 - tli, Le Canadel, NYPL.

4 - 5 to 31 July 1932 - tls; Villa Lauro,
Anacapri; SIU.

4 - 27 August to 20 September 1932 - tls; Hotel
Chabrol, Brantôme, Dordogne; SIU.

2 - 2 and 17 September 1932 - apcs, Brantôme, SIU.

1 - 20 October 1932 - als, Brantôme, SIU.

3 - 9 and 25 November, 10 December 1932 - tls,
    Lisbon, SIU, letter 10 December + tls to
    Aldington from Carlo Cunata, "13 December,"
    Milan.

1 - 25 November 1932 - als, Lisbon, SIU.

1 - 16 December 1932 - apcs, Bordeaux, SIU.

4 - 3 January to 18 March 1933 - tls, St. James's
    Street, SIU, letter 3 March + tls to Aldington
    from Lillian Glaser of 23 February.

31 - 20 March to 17 September 1933 - tls,
    Pramousquier, SIU, letter 20 August + tls to
    Aldington from Doubleday, Doran and Company
    dated 10 August 1933, Garden City, N.Y.

5 - 29 September 1933 to 4 October 1934 - tls; Hotel
    Chateau-Trompette, Bordeaux; SIU.

1 - 10 November 1933 - als; Cascaro (?), Portugal;
    SIU.

1 - 20 November 1933 - als, Gibralter, SIU.

9 - 25 December 1933 to 27 April 1934 - tls; Carlton
    Court, Pall Mall Place, London; SIU.

1 - 30 April 1934 - als, on board [S.S.] *The Royal
    Main Liner,* SIU.

1 - 19 May 1934 - apcs; Leon, Spain; SIU.

2 - 26 May 1934 (2) - tls, Madrid, SIU.

1 - 5 June 1934 - tls, Berne, SIU.

7 - 26 June to 19 September 1934 - als; Spital,
    Feldkirch, Austria; SIU.

9 - 27 July to 4 September 1934 - tls; Pension
    Edelweiss, Fontenella im Grosswalsterstal,
    Voralsberg, Austria; SIU, letter of 4 September
    + als to Aldington from Marie Conovaggio, dated
    28 August 1934, Villa des Pins.

3 - 13 November, 5 and 28 December 1934 - tls;

Georgian House, Bury Street, [London]; SIU.

1 - "Saturday" [1934] - als, n.p., SIU.

Plank, George W.; 13 letters

1 - "Thursday" - als; BEF (Portland, [Dorset]); YU-P.

1 - n.d. [1 February 1915] - ali, Hampstead, YU-P
(on *The Egoist* letterhead.)

1 - n.d. [10 February 1915] - apci, Hampstead, YU-P.

1 - 18 September 1915 - tli, Hampstead, YU-P.

1 - "Weds" [15 November 1916] - als; BEF (Portland,
Dorset); YU-P.

1 - 27 November 1916 - als; BEF (Portland, Dorset);
YU-P.

1 - n.d. [13 December 1917] - als, Mecklenburg
Square, YU-P.

1 - "Sat." - als, n.p., YU-P, + apcs from T. Sturge
Moore dated 14 December 1917 and addressed to
Aldington.

1 - n.d. [19 December 1917] - ali, Mecklenburg Square,
YU-P.

1 - 3 January 1918 - als; BEF (Newhaven, Sussex);
YU-P.

1 - 15 October 1929 - tls; c/o Barclays Bank, Paris;
YU-P.

1 - 28 January 1930 - tls, Tunis, YU-P.

1 - 7 June 1934 - tls, Bern, YU-P.

Politzer, Ronald J. (Williams Collins, publishers);
6 letters

5 - 18 December 1953 to 7 May 1954 - tl, Montpellier,
SIU.

1 - 12 May 1954 - tls, Montpellier, SIU.

Pollard, Marjorie; 7 letters

1 - 2 April 1933 - als, Pramousquier, SIU.

5 - 16 April to 15 August 1933 - tls, Pramousquier,

SIU.

1 - 27 November 1933 - als; Alicante, Spain; SIU.

Pound, Ezra (American poet; discovered and encouraged many
        other poets; editor, essayist, critic. Imagist,
        Vorticist. Lived most of adult life abroad);
        137 letters

[Hamilton and Kirkland Colleges, Clinton, New York,
have correspondence to Pound of the St. Elizabeth
years which is not legally available at present.]

1 - 27 June 1918 - ali, BEF, YU-P.

2 - 23 July 1918 and 14 February 1919 - als; BEF (9th
    Royal Sussex); YU.

6 - 18 August 1918 to 9 February 1919 - als, n.p.
    [BEF], YU.

1 - 14 September 1918 - als, BEF (8th Corps Signal
    School), YU.

3 - 11, 13 and 17 March 1919 - als, London [Authors'
    Club], YU.

1 - 21 July 1919 - als, Littoral, YU.

4 - 29 December 1919 to 20 July 1920 - als, Hermitage,
    YU, + autograph poem: "Any Georgian (In Memoriam
    E.M.)," with 29 December, + autograph copy by
    Aldington of Pound's "Quia Pauper Amavi" with 2
    April 1920 letter.

2 - 16 June and 29 July 1920 - tls, Hermitage, YU.

1 - n.d. [1920?] - tls (top half of letter ripped
    off), n.p., YU.

1 - "Friday 28" [early 1920s?] - als, n.p. [Paris], YU.

1 - n.d. [early 1920s?] - als, n.p., YU.

28 - 21 November 1924 to 14 August 1928 - tls,
    Padworth, YU.

1 - 27th (no month or year)- tls, Paris, YU.

1 - n.d. - als, Anacapri, YU.

1 - 15 February 1926 - als, Padworth, YU.

1 - 6 March 1926 - tls (in French), Padworth, YU.

1 - 6 March 1926 - tls (in French) copy, Padworth, UT.

1 - 11 February 1927 - al (not addressed but written
   by Aldington to the editor of *Exile*), Padworth, YU.

1 - 27 March 1928 - apcs, n.p. (postmark illegible),
   YU.

1 - 7 August 1928 - tls, Padworth, SIU.

1 - 11 September 1928 - apcs, Florence, YU.

2 - 30 September and [1 October 1928] - apcs, Naples,
   YU.

1 - n.d. [1928?] - tls, Rome, YU.

2 - 15 and 18 September 1928 - tls, Rome, YU.

1 - n.d. [October or November 1928] - als; La Vigie,
   Ile de Port-Cros, Var, France; YU.

2 - 4 and 29 December 1928 - als, Paris, YU.

8 - 9 December 1928 to 1 December 1930 - tls, Paris,
   YU.

1 - 21 December 1928 - tls, Paris, YU, + "confidential
   copy" of Aldington's review of English edition
   of Pound's poems.

1 - 5 January 1929 - als, Genoa, YU.

1 - n.d. [1929?] - radiogram, Genoa, YU.

1 - 30 December 1929 - tls, Palermo, YU.

2 - 29 January and 3 February 1930 - tls, Tunis, YU.

1 - 19 February 1930 - tls, Algiers, YU.

3 - 6 July, 22 August 1930 and 14 December 1937 - tls,
   Le Canadel, YU.

1 - 22 October 1930 - apcs, Venice, YU.

2 - 21 January 1931 and n.d. [1931] - als with notes
   to Pound from Norman Douglas and Diere Schutz on
   the same page, n.p., YU.

1 - 4 February 1931 - tls, Florence, YU.

    1 - n.d. [1931] - tpcs, Florence, YU.

    1 - 14 September 1934 - tls, Dordogne, YU.

    1 - 24 January 1938 - tls, Le Canadel, YU, + clipping.

    1 - n.d. [1940?] - tls, Old Lyme, YU.

  17 - 20 June 1951 to 21 July 1957 - tls, Montpellier,
     YU.

    1 - 5 September 1953 - tls, Montpellier, YU, +
     clipping pasted on.

  22 - 18 August 1957 to 17 August 1960 - tls, Sury, YU.

    1 - 29 September 1958 - tls, Sury, YU, + carbon copy
     signed.

    1 - 5 January 1959 - als, Montpellier, YU.

    1 - n.d. - als, n.p., YU.

Powell, Lawrence Clark (librarian, University of Southern
               California, Los Angeles; author
               lecturer; essayist); 60 letters

  18 - 14 September 1944 to 27 December 1945 - tls,
     Hollywood, UCLA.

    1 - 18 May 1946 - als, Jamaica, UCLA.

    2 - 2 June and 5 July 1946 - tls, Jamaica, UCLA.

    1 - 28 July 1946 - tls; c/o Royal Bank of Canada,
     Montego Bay, Jamaica; YU.

    2 - 3 and 18 September 1946 - tls; c/o American
     Express, Paris; UCLA.

    1 - 21 October 1946 - tls, Raspail, UCLA.

    1 - 3 [or 30] December 1946 - tls, Montparnasse, UCLA.

  27 - 17 August 1947 to 2 November 1950 - tls, Le
     Lavandou, UCLA.

    6 - 3 March 1958 to 19 July 1962 - tls, Sury, UCLA.

    1 - n.d. - apcs, n.p., UCLA.

Prentice, C. H. C. (editor, Chatto & Windus; friend of
               Aldington, Orioli and Douglas; retired
               early to enjoy archaeology in Greece);

2 letters

1 - 18 November 1930 - tls; c/o Barclays Bank, Paris; SIU.

1 - 6 June 1952 - tl, Montpellier, SIU.

Prokosch, Frederic (American writer, poet and novelist); 1 letter

1 - 17 September 1930 - tls; c/o Barclays Bank, Paris; TU.

Putnam, Samuel (American writer, biographer, translator, critic); 1 letter

1 - 21 June 1928 - tls; Rue Vauquelin, [Paris]; SIU.

Rago, Henry (poet, editor, educator; editor *Poetry: A Magazine of Verse*); 3 letters

3 - 25 June, 10 October 1956 and 15 January 1957 - tls, Montpellier, UC.

Randall, Sir Alec (British diplomat; writer; once secretary to Ford Madox Ford and friend of Aldington from those days); 33 letters

1 - 2 June 1918 - als, BEF [Western Front], HL.

1 - 17 April 1924 - als, Padworth, HL.

3 - 28 November 1925, 10 and 23 August 1927 - tls, Padworth, HL.

2 - 23 April 1928 and 29 September 1930 - tls, Paris, HL.

1 - 13 October 1928 - als; La Vigie, Ile de Port-Cros, Var; HL.

1 - 16 June 1933 - tls, Pramousquier, HL.

14 - 4 December 1953 to 25 June 1957 - tls, Montpellier, HL.

9 - 23 August 1957 to 10 March 1961 - tls, Sury, HL.

1 - 3 November 1961 - tls, Aix-en-Provence, HL.

Rankin, General G. J. (Australian representative and senator; served in both World Wars;

> commanded 4th Australian Light Horse
> in World War I); 1 letter

1 - 20 August 1957 - tls, Sury, SIU.

Rappaport, Herman A.; 12 letters

1 - 1952 [December] - Christmas card with written
   message, n.p., SIU.

9 - 3 December 1953 to 24 February 1957 - tls,
   Montpellier, UCLA.

2 - 6 February and 2 May 1958 - tls, Sury, UCLA.

Ravagli, Angelo (Italian army officer; third husband of
   Frieda Lawrence); 3 letters

2 - 1 and 8 February 1941 - tls, Washington, UT.

1 - 14 August 1956 - tls, Montpellier, UT.

Ray, [Roy?], Lewis; 1 letter

1 - 18 June 1921 - als, Padworth, NU.

Read, Sir Herbert (English poet, publisher, art critic;
   lecturer at University of Edinburgh,
   University of Liverpool and Harvard.
   Helped produce *Criterion*. Thirty-five of
   these letters were published by Professor
   David S. Thatcher in "Richard Aldington's
   letters to Herbert Read," *The Malahat
   Review*, 15 [July 1970], 5-44); 70 letters

1 - 13 January 1919 - als, "Ex vinculus," UVI.

1 - 28 March 1919 - als, Authors' Club, UVI.

1 - 16 April 1923 - als, Padworth, UVI.

40 - 3 September 1924 to 7 October 1927 - tls,
   Padworth, UVI.

3 - 15 July 1929, 24 June and 27 November 1930 - tls;
   c/o Barclays Bank, Paris, UVI.

1 - 25 July 1929 - tls; Hotel Rivage de Fabrégas,
   Fabrégas, La Seyne, Var; UVI.

2 - 9 August and 15 September 1930 - tls; Villa le

Bouquet, Aiguebelle, par Le Lavandou, Var; UVI.

2 - 30 May and 5 June 1931 - tls, Le Canadel, UVI.

1 - 14 January 1933 - tls, St. James's St., UVI.

4 - 3 April to 13 July 1933 - tls, Pramousquier, UVI.

2 - 22 and 31 December 1934 - tls; Georgian House,
    Bury St. [London]; UVI.

1 - 25 February 1936 - tls; Cavendish House, Jermyn
    St., [London]; UVI.

2 - 19 January and 7 March 1946 - tls, Hollywood, UVI.

1 - 27 June 1946 - tls; c/o Royal Bank of Canada,
    Montego Bay, Jamaica; UVI.

7 - 29 March 1956 to 12 March 1957 - tls, Montpellier,
    UVI.

1 - 28 October 1961 - tls, Aix-en-Provence, UVI.

le Redacteur en chef, *Revue de Paris;* 1 letter

1 - 15 March 1955 - tl (carbon), Montpellier, NYPL.

Reeves, James (poet, anthologist. These letters have been
        published by Professor Miriam J. Benkovitz
        in "Nine for Reeves," *The Bulletin of the
        New York Public Library,* 69 [June 1965],
        349-74); 9 letters

2 - 13 May and 7 June 1930 - tls; Ursulines;
    Professor Miriam J. Benkovitz, c/o Skidmore
    College, Saratoga Springs, New York.

2 - 8 and 18 November 1930 - tls; c/o Barclays Bank,
    Paris; Professor Miriam J. Benkovitz, c/o Skidmore
    College, Saratoga Springs, New York.

2 - 5 March 1931 and 17 February 1932 - tls; Florence;
    Professor Miriam J. Benkovitz, c/o Skidmore
    College, Saratoga Springs, New York.

1 - 26 May 1931 - tls; Le Canadel; Professor Miriam
    J. Benkovitz, c/o Skidmore College, Saratoga
    Springs, New York.

1 - 10 November 1932 - tls; Lisbon; Professor Miriam
J. Benkovitz, c/o Skidmore College, Saratoga
Springs, New York.

1 - 6 March 1933 - tls; Pramousquier; Professor
Miriam J. Benkovitz, c/o Skidmore College,
Saratoga Springs, New York.

Roditi, Georges (*Directeur litterarie des Editions,*
Amiot-Dumont, publishers); 2 letters

1 - 15 October 1954 - copy dated and signed by
Aldington, Montpellier; Collection of Raymond
and Peggy Sturge, Bournemouth, England.

1 - 15 October 1954 - tl (carbon), Montpellier, NYPL.

Rugg, Harold Goddard (assistant librarian at Dartmouth
College); 2 letters

1 - 30 November 1922 - als, Padworth, D.

1 - 19 February 1939 - als, New York City, D.

Russell, Peter (bookseller, publisher, admirer of Pound);
8 letters

1 - 5 January 1950 - tls, Le Lavandou, SUNY.

4 - 18 December 1951 to 29 July 1952 - tls,
Montpellier, SUNY.

1 - 13 March 1955 - tls, Montpellier, NYPL.

1 - 14 May 1956 - tls, Montpellier, SIU.

1 - 16 September 1959 - tls, Sury, SIU.

Sadleir, Michael (Constable & Company, publishers);
2 letters

1 - 27 January 1929 - tls; c/o Barclays Bank, Paris
[Naples]; TU.

1 - 9 March 1930 - tls; c/o Barclays Bank, Paris; TU.

Sanderson, Cobden; 1 letter

1 - 30 June 1919 - als, Littoral, SUNY.

Schiff, Sydney (novelist; short-story writer under the
pseudonym of Stephen Hudson); 35 letters

1 - 25 May 1930 - tls, Ursulines, BM.

1 - 13 July 1930 - tls; le Bouquet, Aiguebelle, par
    Le Lavandou, Var; BM.

1 - 16 October 1930 - tls, Venice, BM.

9 - 23 December 1930 to 2 May 1932 - tls, Florence,
    BM.

1 - 26 March 1931 - als, Amalfi, BM.

1 - 23 April 1931 - als, Munich, BM.

6 - 14 May 1931 to 7 March 1938 - tls, Le Canadel,
    BM.

1 - 29 October 1931 - apcs, Mainz, BM.

1 - 3 October 1932 - als ("lettercard"); 26
    Porchester Square, London; BM.

1 - 17 October 1932 - apcs; Sées, Orne; BM.

1 - 19 November 1932 - tls, Lisbon, BM.

1 - 25 December 1932 - tls; c/o Ralph Pinker,
    London; BM.

2 - 19 January and 20 February 1933 - tls, St. James's
    St., BM.

1 - 31 December 1934 - tls, London, BM.

7 - 21 January 1949 to 14 June 1950 - tls, Le
    Lavandou, BM.

Secker, Martin (publisher); 9 letters

6 - 7 March 1934 to 25 January 1935 - tls, London,
    UTO.

3 - 21 March, 27 April and 13 May 1953 - tls,
    Montpellier, TU.

Sitwell, Osbert (poet, satirist, essayist, short-story
                  writer, author of reminiscences); 2 letters

1 - 24 November 1919 - als, Authors' Club, BU.

1 - 19 August 1920 - als, Hermitage, UT.

Slonimsky, Dr. Henry (Polish-American philosopher,
                      professor at Jewish Institute of

Religion, New York City); 92 letters

2 - [3 and 17 November 1913] - als, Kensington, SIU.

3 - 2, 14 and 25 July 1927 - als, Padworth, SIU.

1 - 23 July 1927 - apcs, Florence, SIU.

3 - 12 and 31 August 1927, 11 May 1928 - tls,
     Padworth, SIU.

1 - 6 September 1927 - apcs, n.p., SIU.

3 - 20 February, 17 September 1929 and 11 August
     1931 - tls; c/o Barclays Bank, Paris; SIU, 17
     September letter + photograph of Aldington.

1 - 8 September 1931 - tls, Le Canadel, SIU.

1 - 7 June 1932 - tls, Anacapri, SIU.

1 - 9 April 1933 - tls, Pramousquier, SIU.

2 - 10 and 23 September 1935 - tls, Old Lyme, SIU.

1 - 2 January 1937 - tls; Yemasse, South Carolina;
     SIU.

1 - 7 January 1937 - tls, New York City, SIU.

6 - 7 April to 19 September 1939 - tls; Peace Dale,
     Rhode Island; SIU.

2 - 12 May and 21 June 1939 - tls; Saunderstown,
     Rhode Island; SIU.

7 - 26 September 1939 to 5 June 1940 - tls, New York
     City, SIU.

6 - 11 July to 23 October 1940 - tls, Old Lyme, SIU.

1 - 8 November 1940 - tls; Hotel Continental,
     Washington, D.C.; SIU.

5 - 22 November 1940 to 10 February 1941 - tls,
     Washington, SIU.

15 - 19 April 1941 to 12 August 1942 - tls, Jamay
     SIU.

1 - 30 June 1941 - tls; Kiowa Ranch, San Cristobal,
     New Mexico; SIU.

24 - 15 January 1943 to 14 March 1945 - tls, Hollywood,

SIU.

1 - 14 August 1946 - als; Park Avenue, New York City;
        SIU.

1 - 15 September 1946 - als; Rue Scribe, Paris; SIU.

1 - 8 July 1947 - tls, Montparnasse, SIU.

1 - 19 December 1949 - tls, Le Lavandou, SIU.

1 - 15 December 1952 - cable, Montpellier, SIU.

Slonimsky, Mrs. Henry (Miriam, wife of above); 30 letters

1 - 23 December 1941 - tls, Jamay, SIU, + two
        photographs of Catherine.

1 - 26 December 1943 - tls, Hollywood, SIU.

6 - 24 April 1948 to 29 January 1949 - tls, Le
        Lavandou, SIU.

20 - 12 December 1951 to 15 January 1955 - tls,
        Montpellier, SIU, 17 February 1952 + bank check.

2 - 19 October and 9 November 1959 - tls, Sury, SIU.

Snow, Lord [C. P.] (physicist, government official,
                essayist, novelist); 1 letter

1 - 30 April 1947 - tls, Montparnasse, UT.

Squire, Sir John Collings (journalist, poet; editor of
                *New Statesman, London Mercury,
                Georgian Poets*); 3 letters

3 - 14 and 21 May, 11 November 1927 - tls, Padworth,
        UCLA.

Steele, Mr.; 2 letters

2 - 6 and 15 August 1930 - tls; Le Bouquet
        [Aiguebelle, par Le Lavandou, Var]; SIU, letter
        6 August + clipping *Daily Mail and Empire* of 21
        June 1930.

Sternberg, Vernon (director, Southern Illinois University
                Press); 11 letters

10 - 16 January to 10 June 1960 - tls, Sury, SIU, +
        10 August 1960 tls Michael Urnov to Aldington.

1 - 28 April 1961 - als, "as from Sury but from
    Venice," SIU.

Storrs, Sir Ronald (English diplomat; accompanied T. E.
                 Lawrence on first trip to Hejaz;
                 governor of Jerusalem); 1 letter

1 - 27 March 1955 - tls, Montpellier, SIU.

Strassman, Miss (Viking Press, Inc.); 3 letters

1 - 13 August 1940 - tls, Old Lyme, V.

2 - 10 Ocotber and 16 December 1943 - tls, Hollywood,
    V.

Taylor, Rachel Annand (journalist, poet, biographer;
                 student of Renaissance); 2 letters

1 - 6 January 1950 - tls, Le Lavandou, NYPL.

1 - 2 July 1952 - Montpellier, NYPL.

Temple, F.-J. (French poet, critic, translator, editor,
          and student of English literature; director
          of Programs, Radiodiffusion-Television
          Française, Montpellier); 118 letters

18 - 12 May 1954 to 7 January 1957 - tls (in French),
     Montpellier, T.

10 - 1 June 1954 to 27 April 1955 - tls, Montpellier, T.

1 - 3 August 1954 - tls, Le Lavandou, T.

1 - 19 August 1954 - tli, Le Lavandou, T.

1 - 25 February 1955 - tli, Montpellier, T.

1 - 2 December 1955 - apci (in French), Montpellier,
    T.

1 - 8 April 1956 - als (in French), Montpellier, T.

1 - 1 July 1957 - tli (in French), Montpellier, T.

1 - 27 July 1957 - apci (in French), Riom, T.

36 - 5 September 1957 to 9 June 1962 - tls, Sury, T.

23 - 9 September 1957 to 8 November 1960 - tls
     (in French), Sury, T.

3 - 8 November 1957, 31 March 1959 and 8 March 1960

- tls (in French and English), Sury, T.

1 - 30 November 1959 - apcs (in French), Vezélay sent
     from Sury, T.

1 - 10 December 1959 - apcs, Sury, T.

1 - 6 January 1961 - apcs, Aix-en-Provence, T.

11 - 17 January 1961 to 19 February 1962 - tls, Aix-
     en-Provence, T.

1 - 30 March 1961 - tls (in French), Saintes, T.

1 - 13 April 1961 - apcs (in French), Cannes, T.

1 - 17 April 1961 - apcs, Venice, T.

1 - 10 May 1961 - apcs (in French), Venice, T.

1 - 10 May 1961 - apci (in French), Venice, T.

1 - 19 June 1961 - apcs (some lines in English signed
     "Richard" and some in French signed by Alister
     Kershaw and his wife), Sury, T.

1 - 25 June 1962 - apcs (in French), Moscow, T.

Tewson, W. Orton (literary editor Philadelphia *Public
                    Ledger* 1921-26; editor *Literary Review*
                    of the New York *Evening Post* 1924-26);
                    2 letters

2 - 18 August and 3 September 1924 - tls, Padworth,
     UV.

Theis, Louise Morgan (journalist, editor, published under
                    the name of "Morgan"); 30 letters

1 - 22 November 1929 - tli, Rome, NYPL.

6 - 12 March to 27 June 1930 - tls, Paris, NYPL.

1 - 15 March 1930 - apcs, Paris, NYPL.

1 - 21 August 1930 - tls, Le Lavandou, NYPL.

4 - 22 January to 31 March 1931 - tls, Florence, NYPL.

1 - 17 February 1931 - als, Florence, NYPL.

1 - 22 March 1931 - apcs, Salerno, NYPL.

1 - 20 February 1933 - als, St. James's St., NYPL.

1 - 15 March 1933 - tls, St. James's St., NYPL.

1 - 21 March 1933 - apcs; Gournay-en-Bray, Seine,
     France; NYPL.

11 - 27 March 1933 to 15 July 1933 - tls, Le Lavandou,
     NYPL.

1 - 11 August 1934 -.tls; Vorarlberg, Austria; NYPL.

Thompson, Mr.; 1 letter

1 - 31 January 1956 - tls, Montpellier, SIU.

Tietjens, Eunice (American poet and novelist; editor;
                    journalist; writer of autobiography;
                    3 letters

1 - 6 June 1923 - tls, Padworth, NE.

2 - 19 June and 12 September 1923 - apcs, Padworth,
     NE.

Tindall, William York (professor at Columbia University;
                    literary scholar, critic); 3 letters

3 - 5 April to 26 July 1940 - tls, New York City,
     CO.

Titus, Edward W. (Paris bookseller and publisher: The Sign
                of the Black Manikin); 20 letters

1 - 28 October 1929 - als, Corneille, UT.

4 - 29 October 1929 to 28 March 1930 - tls, Corneille,
     UT.

1 - 20 December 1929 - tls, Palermo, UT.

1 - 3 January 1930 - apci, Tunis, UT.

2 - 11 and 27 January 1930 - tls, Tunis, UT.

1 - 28 March 1930 - tli, Corneille, UT.

2 - 26 May and 25 June 1930 - tls, Ursulines, UT.

2 - 29 June and 1 December 1930 - tls; c/o Barclays
     Bank, Paris; UT.

5 - 14 May to 29 August 1931 - tls, Le Canadel, UT.

1 - 31 May 1932 - tls, Anacapri, UT.

Udell, Miss; 1 letter

1 - 22 June 1937 - tls, London, UC.

Unidentified Recipients, 10 letters

    1 - 30 November 1918 - als, n.p. [London], YU.

    1 - 4 December 1929 - tls; c/o Barclays Bank, Paris
        [written from Sorrento]; SIU.

    1 - 11 November 1932 - tl copy; c/o Thomas Cook & Son,
        Libson, Portugal; SIU.

    1 - 28 September 1955 - tl carbon copy first page
        only, Montpellier, SIU.

    1 - n.d. - als, London, YU.

    1 - n.d. - tl, n.p., NYPL.

    1 - n.d. - tls (first page[s] missing), n.p., SIU.

    1 - n.d. - als (first page[s] missing), n.p., UT.

    1 - n.d. - tl, carbon copy of pages 2 and 3 only, n.p.,
        SIU.

    1 - n.d. - tl, carbon copy of page 3 only, n.p., SIU.

Untermeyer, Louis (American poet, editor, anthologist);
                      3 letters

    2 - 25 November 1919 and 4 January 1920 - als,
        Authors' Club, IU.

    1 - 19 February 1923 - als, Padworth, IU.

Urnov, Mikhail V. (Russian professor, critic and scholar;
              connected with Foreign Commission of
              USSR, Writers' Union); 39 letters

    8 - 19 April 1956 to 22 July 1957 - tls, Montpellier,
        recipient.

    29 - 12 September 1957 to 15 July 1962 - tls, Sury,
        recipient.

    1 - 6 January 1961 - apcs, Aix-en-Provence, recipient.

    1 - 7 January 1961 - tls, Aix-en-Provence, recipient.

Van Doren, Irita (literary editor New York *Herald Tribune*
              1926-63); 3 letters

    2 - 9 January and 16 March 1929 - tls; c/o Barclays
        Bank, Paris; LC.

1 - 24 December 1934 - tls; c/o Chatto & Windus,
    London; LC.

Van Patten, Nathan (professor at Stanford University);
                    7 letters

7 - 26 June 1948 to 17 April 1951 - tls, Le Lavandou,
    SIU, + typescript poem intended for a memorial
    service for Stanford's war dead.

Vincendon, Claude; 13 letters

7 - 24 March 1958 to 13 June 1962 - tls, Sury, SIU.

4 - 13 December 1960 to 22 February 1962 - tls,
    Aix-en-Provence, SIU.

2 - 12 and 17 May 1961 - apcs, Venice, SIU.

Walters, Miss (William Heinemann, Ltd.); 5 letters

5 - 18 August 1955 to 27 February 1957 - tls,
    Montpellier, H.

Warman, Eric (novelist, publisher, writer of detective
                    stories); 268 letters

1 - 1 April 1932 - tls, Florence, SIU.

1 - 21 May 1932 - tls, Anacapri, SIU.

1 - 16 March 1933 - tls; c/o Ralph Pinker, London;
    SIU.

1 - 17 May 1933 - tls, Pramousquier, SIU.

1 - 15 August 1933 - tli, Pramousquier, SIU.

1 - 21 October 1933 - tls; Gran Hotel Londres, Madrid;
    SIU.

2 - 12 December 1933 and 4 January 1934 - tli;
    Carlton Court, Pall Mall Place, London; SIU.

1 - 31 December 1933 - als; Carlton Court, Pall Mall
    Place, London; SIU.

1 - 6 June 1934 - tli, Berne, SIU.

1 - 26 September 1934 - tls; c/o Chatto & Windus,
    London; SIU.

1 - 22 April 1936 - als; Washington Irving Hotel,

Grenada; SIU.

1 - 24 May 1936 - als; Collobrières, Var; SIU.

1 - 14 June 1936 - als; Feldkirch, Austria; SIU.

4 - 7 July to 6 September 1936 - tls; Alpenhotel,
Fernpass in Tirol, Austria; SIU.

1 - 18 September 1936 - tls; chez Monsieur Lugon, Le
Lavandou, Var; SIU.

13 - 17 April 1937 to 9 November 1938 - tls, Le
Canadel, SIU.

1 - 23 October 1937 - als, Boulogne-Sur-Mer, SIU.

1 - 29 October 1937 - tls; Ashley Bank, Pinner Hill,
Middlesex; SIU.

2 - 20 and 28 May 1938 - tls; Pully, Lausanne; SIU.

1 - 2 July 1938 - tls; Astor Hotel, Princes Square,
London; SIU.

4 - 25 July to 24 August 1938 - tls; Bramshott Cottage,
Woolmer Lane, Liphook, Hants.; SIU.

7 - 5 June 1939 to 16 August 1942 - tls; c/o Viking
Press, East 48th St., New York City; SIU.

1 - 3 August 1939 - tls; The Scallop Shell, Peace
Dale, Rhode Island; SIU.

4 - 9 July to 17 October 1940 - tls, Old Lyme, SIU.

1 - 15 February 1941 - tls, Washington, SIU.

6 - 11 March 1941 to 9 April 1942 - tls, Jamay, SIU,
11 March 1941 letter + tls from Mechanical-
Copyright Protection Society, Ltd., to Aldington
dated 3 February 1941.

18 - 30 December 1942 to 10 April 1946 - tls,
Hollywood, SIU.

2 - 8 and 17 June 1946 - tls, Jamaica, SIU.

1 - 1 September 1946 - tls; c/o American Express,
Rue Scribe, Paris; SIU.

2 - 14 September and 13 December 1946 - tls, Raspail,

SIU.

5 - 25 January to 5 July 1947 - tls, Montparnasse,
     SIU.

9 - 11 August 1947 to 22 September 1950 - tls, Le
     Lavandou, SIU.

1 - 22 September 1950 - telegram, Le Lavandou, SIU.

85 - 2 August 1952 to 29 June 1957 - tls, Montpellier,
     SIU, 8 May 1954 + tls from Frieda Lawrence to
     Aldington dated 29 March 1954 from Texas; 15 June
     1954 + extract from al from H. D. to Aldington
     dated 8 June 1954; 4 February 1955 + extract from
     letter from Roy Campbell received 4 February 1955;
     10 November 1956 + tls re: Aldington's finances;
     7 January 1957 + news clipping; 12 March 1957 +
     tls from Boris Izakov, USSR.

1 - 24 November 1954 - als, n.p., SIU.

1 - 5 April 1955 - apcs, Saintes, SIU.

1 - 3 February 1956 - telegram, Montpellier, SIU.

70 - 28 October 1957 to 25 July 1962 - tls, Sury, SIU,
     9 January 1958 + carbon copy report; 24 August
     1959 + tls Aldington to Mr. Wood dated 22 August
     1959 (not sent to addressee); 19 September 1959
     + pamphlet; 2 December 1959 + news clipping;
     29 January 1960 + tls from M. Urnov to Aldington
     dated 28 January 1960 from Moscow; 24 February
     1960 + pamphlet; 3 October 1960 + carbon extract
     2 pp.; 10 October 1960 + magazine clipping; 30
     May 1962 + tls from Alexie Surkoo to Aldington
     from Moscow dated 9 February 1962; 17 July 1962
     letter + translation of address to Aldington in
     Moscow, 8 July 1962; 25 July 1962 + news clipping.

1 - 3 April 1958 - telegram; St. Satur, Cher; SIU.

1 - 19 December 1960 - apcs, Rome, SIU.

1 - 14 May 1929 - tls; c/o Barclays Bank, Paris; SUNY.

1 - 5 June 1929 - tls, Select, SUNY.

2 - 7 June and 13 July 1929 - tls; c/o Barclays Bank, Paris; SUNY.

1 - 20 August 1929 - tls, Paris, YU.

1 - 25 November 1929 - tls; c/o Barclays Bank, Paris [written from Naples]; SUNY, + letter 15 November 1929 from Chatto & Windus to Aldington.

1 - 5 December 1929 - tls, Paris, SUNY.

Williamson, Henry (British novelist; journalist); 1 letter

1 - 5 October 1950 - als, Saint-Tropez, SIU.

Woolf, Virginia (novelist, essayist, critic; prominent Bloomsburyite); 1 letter

1 - 22 September 1923 - als, Padworth, NYPL.

Wreden, William P. (American bookdealer and publisher); 2 letters

2 - 15 September 1948 and 21 February 1949 - tls, Le Lavandou, SIU.

Wright, [?]; 1 letter

1 - 20 July 1962 - tls, Sury, TU.

Yale, William (American historian; participated prominently in the Paris Peace Conference after World War I; taught at the University of New Hampshire); 1 letter

1 - 7 November 1955 - tls photocopy, Montpellier, BU.

Young, Jessica Brett (singer; wife of Francis Brett Young, English novelist); 1 letter

1 - 2 September 1958 - tls, Sury, UB.

Zhantieva, Dilyara (Russian professor, critic and scholar); 27 letters

1 - n.d. - apcs, Venice, estate of Professor Zhantieva.

2 - 6 March and 23 April 1957 - tls, Montpellier,

estate of Professor Zhantieva.

20 - 9 March 1959 to 18 July 1962 - tls, Sury, estate
      of Professor Zhantieva.

 1 - 4 January 1961 - apcs, Sury, estate of Professor
      Zhantieva.

 1 - 2 May 1961 - als, Venice, estate of Professor
      Zhantieva.

 2 - 30 October 1961 and 26 January 1962 - tls, Aix-
      en-Provence, estate of Professor Zhantieva.

5

A Chronology of Aldington's Addresses

The span of dates preceding each address indicates simply
the earliest and latest dates (month and year) when these
addresses were used by Aldington on letters included in this
Checklist. A comparison with the Chronology of Aldington's
Travels, which follows, will indicate that he sometimes
lived at the same address (Villa Koeclin, Le Canadel, Var,
France, for instance) intermittently. Only a careful
examination of the letters themselves, including letters
missing here and other biographical data, could produce a
complete chronology of Aldington's life. This does not
purport to be more than a compilation from the dates and
addresses shown on the letters listed.

```
12/1911 - Twickenham
8/1913 to 12/1914 - Kensington
5/1914 to 2/1916 - Hampstead
1/1916 to 1/1919 - BEF
3 to 6/1916 - Woodland Cottage
6/1917 to 4/1918 - Mecklenburg Square
12/1918 to 6/1920 - Rye and Authors' Club
2/1919 to 11/1920 - Hermitage, Authors' Club, Littoral
12/1920 to 8/1928 - Padworth
6/1928 to 12/1930 - Select, Notre Dame, and Corneille
3 to 11/1930 - Ursulines
7/1930 to 1/1939 - Le Canadel
4 to 8/1933 - Pramousquier
3 to 5/1935 - Tobago
7/1935 to 10/1940 - Old Lyme; Peace Dale and
                         Saundersfield, R.I.; New York
```

City

11/1940 to 2/1941 - Washington

2/1941 to 9/1942 - Jamay

9/1942 to 4/1946 - Hollywood

5 to 7/1946 - Jamaica

9/1946 to 7/1947 - Raspail and Montparnasse

7/1947 to 4/1951 - Le Lavandou

5/1951 to 7/1957 - Montpellier

8/1957 to 7/1962 - Sury

10/1960 to 5/1962 - Aix-en-Provence

6

A Chronology of Aldington's Travels

This chronology does not include local trips but only longer journeys or journeys outside the country of his residence at the time. It is often difficult to decide whether on a particular date the place given should be considered as a "travel address" or a "principal address." Decisions, of necessity, have been arbitrary, and both this and the preceding chronology should be consulted simultaneously with the reservation previously noted regarding the data underlying both tables.

May to June 1912 - Paris
December 1912 - Rome
March to June 1913 - Anacapri; Florence; Venice; Verona;
                               Lago di Garda
July 1913 - Paris
September 1922 - Italy
May 1924 - Italy
April 1927 - Paris
July 1927 - Florence
June 1928 - Paris
September 1928 - Florence; Naples; Rome
October to November 1928 - La Vigie, Ile de Port-Cros, Var
December 1928 - London; Isle of Thanet
January and February 1929 - Genoa; Rapallo
June 1929 - Palermo
July to September 1929 - Hotel Rivage de Fabrégas,
                               Fabrégas, La Seyne, Var
November to December 1929 - Rome; Naples; Amalfi;
                               Palermo; Sorrento

January to February 1930 - Tunisia; Algeria

April 1930 - London

July to September 1930 - Le Bouquet, Aiguebelle, par Le
                         Lavandou, Var

September to December 1930 - Venice; Lecce; Florence;
                             Brindisi; Palermo

February to March 1931 - Florence; Amalfi; Salerno

April to October 1931 - Germany

January to August 1932 - Florence; Anacapri

September to October 1932 - London

September to December 1932 - Lisbon; Bordeaux; Brantôme;
                             Sées

January to March 1933 - 4 Palace Chambers, 24 St. James's
                         St., London

March 1933 - Gournay-en-Bray, Seine

October to November 1933 - Portugal; Spain; Gibralter

December 1933 to April 1934 - Carlton Court, Pall Mall
                              Place, London

May 1934 - Portugal

June 1934 - Berne

June to September 1934 - Austria

November to December 1934 - London

October 1935 - London

January to March 1936 - London

April 1936 - Granada

June 1936 - Genoa

June to September 1936 - Austria

October 1936 - London

December 1936 - aboard S. S. *Normandie*

January 1937 - Yemassie, South Carolina

February 1937 - London

February to March 1937 - Florence; Capri

June 1937 - London

October to November 1937 - Pinner Hill, Middlesex

May 1938 - Switzerland

June to August 1938 - London; Liphook, Hants.

February 1939 - London

May to July 1941 - San Cristobal, New Mexico

July to December 1942 - Boulder, Colorado

August 1946 - New York City

October 1954 - Paris

December 1954 - Genoa

January 1959 - Monaco

November 1959 - Zurich

August 1960 - Zagreb

December 1960 - Rome

March to May 1961 - Venice

June 1962 - Leningrad

June to July 1962 - Moscow

7

Index to Recipients
and Letter Totals

Bryher, Winifred	240 letters
Bubb, Rev. Charles C.	18 letters
Buck, Michell S.	3 letters
Burke, Mr.	1 letter
Callender, Miss L.	2 letters
Campbell, Mary	2 letters
Campbell, Roy	8 letters
Cape, Jonathan	1 letter
Cate, Garth	1 letter
Church, Richard	11 letters
Cockburn, Frank B.	6 letters
Coghill, [?]	1 letter
Collins, William	4 letters
Constable & Company	3 letters
Cournos, John	34 letters
Covici, Pascal	39 letters
Cunard, Nancy	1 letter
Dahlberg, Edward	10 letters
Davis, Lambert	1 letter
Deasey, W. Denison	161 letters
Dibben, William	201 letters
Dobrée, Mrs. Bonamy (Valentine)	1 letter
Doolittle, Hilda	716 letters
Doran, George H.	3 letters
Douglas, Robin	1 letter
Drake, Lawrence	6 letters
Dujardin, Édouard	1 letter
Durrell, Lawrence	197 letters
Dutton, G. P. H. and Ninette Dutton	220 letters
Dyson, Mr.	2 letters
Eastman, Max	1 letter
Editor, *Atlantic Monthly*	1 letter
Editor, *Daily Telegram*	1 letter

Harrison, Michael	4 letters
Hatch, Mr.	1 letter
William Heinemann, Ltd.	1 letter
Holroyd-Reece, John	5 letters
Horne and Birkett	1 letter
Huebsch, Benjamin W.	2 letters
Hughes, Babette	4 letters
Hughes, Babette and Glenn	6 letters
Hughes, Glenn A.	46 letters
Hunt, Violet	1 letter
Hutchens, Patricia (Mrs. Richard Graesen)	4 letters
Hynes, S. L.	2 letters
Isaac, Elizabeth	1 letter
Jackson, Holbrook	11 letters
Johnson, Martyn	4 letters
Jonas, Klaus, W.	2 letters
Jones, Zuleika	1 letter
Joyce, James	3 letters
Joynson-Hicks & Co.	1 letter
Kershaw, Alister	1201 letters
Kershaw, Shelia	1 letter
Knollenberg, Bernhard	5 letters
Kreymbourg, Alfred	1 letter
Langham, Dr. S. T.	2 letters
Laughlin, Mr.	1 letter
Lawrence, Freida	16 letters
Lawrence, Professor	1 letter
Layton, Mr.	1 letter
Lehmann, John	2 letters
Lewis, Percy Wyndham	23 letters
Loving, Edward Pierre	1 letter
Lowell, Amy	102 letters
Lyle, Rob	102 letters

Pearce, Charles	1 letter
Pearson, Norman Holmes	3 letters
Pinker, James B. and Sons	11 letters
Pinker, J. Ralph	195 letters
Plank, George W.	13 letters
Politzer, Ronald J.	6 letters
Pollard, Marjorie	7 letters
Pound, Ezra	137 letters
Powell, Lawrence Clark	60 letters
Prentice, C. H. C.	2 letters
Prokosch, Fredric	1 letter
Putnam, Samuel	1 letter
Rago, Henry	3 letters
Randall, Sir Alec	33 letters
Rankin, General G. J.	1 letter
Rappaport, Herman A.	12 letters
Ravagli, Angelo	3 letters
Ray, Lewis	1 letter
Read, Sir Herbert	70 letters
le Redacteur en chef, *Revue de Paris*	1 letter
Reeves, James	9 letters
Roditi, Georges	2 letters
Rugg, Harold Goddard	2 letters
Russell, Peter	8 letters
Sadleir, Michael	2 letters
Sanderson, Cobden	1 letter
Schiff, Sydney	35 letters
Secker, Martin	9 letters
Sitwell, Osbert	2 letters
Slonimsky, Dr. Henry	92 letters
Slonimsky, Mrs. Henry (Miriam)	30 letters
Snow, Lord (C. P.)	1 letter
Squire, Sir John Collings	3 letters

Brett Young)   1 letter
Zhantieva, Dilyara   27 letters

Named recipients = 224   7,254 letters

8

Index to Holdings
by Repositories

Private holders are listed with these repositories only if
they hold groups of letters addressed to others as well as
(in some cases) to themselves. For full names of recipients
and other information see "Alphabetical Listing."

Miriam J. Benkovitz	22 letters
Beaumont	1 letter
Harald	9 letters
Harald, Mrs.	1 letter
Langham	2 letters
Reeves	9 letters
British Museum Library	95 letters
Aldington, Netta	60 letters
Schiff	35 letters
Boston University	3 letters
Sitwell	1 letter
Waugh	1 letter
Yale	1 letter
Jonathan Cape Ltd.	1 letter
Cape	1 letter
Columbia University	3 letters
Tindall	3 letters
Cornell University	24 letters
Joyce	1 letter
Lewis	23 letters
Dartmouth College	2 letters
Rugg	2 letters
William Heinemann Ltd.	283 letters
Aldington, P. A. G.	1 letter

Callender	2 letters
Evans, A.	1 letter
Evans, C.	4 letters
Frere	267 letters
Hall	1 letter
Heinemann	1 letter
Noble	1 letter
Walters	5 letters
The Huntington	33 letters
Randall	33 letters
Harvard University	149 letters
Cournos	34 letters
Eliot	12 letters
Jones	1 letter
Lowell	102 letters
Indiana University	11 letters
Eastman	1 letter
Moore, T. Sturge	7 letters
Untermeyer	3 letters
Library of Congress	7 letters
Huebsch	2 letters
MacLeish	2 letters
Van Doren	3 letters
Middlebury College	3 letters
Wilkinson	3 letters
National Library of Australia	156 letters
Deasey	156 letters
The Newberry Library	3 letters
Teitjens	3 letters
Northwestern University	3 letters
Aldis	1 letter
Ray	1 letter
Wilkinson	1 letter

New York University	31 letters
Brown	31 letters
New York Public Library	315 letters
Bird	147 letters
Buck	2 letters
Campbell, R.	4 letters
Editor, *Daily Telegram*	1 letter
Haley	1 letter
Hunt	1 letter
Lyle	102 letters
Marshall	4 letters
Moult	4 letters
Pinker, J. B.	11 letters
Pinker, J. R.	1 letter
le Redacteur en chef, *Revu de Paris*	1 letter
Roditi	1 letter
Russell	1 letter
Taylor	2 letters
Theis	30 letters
Unidentified	1 letter
Woolf	1 letter
Estate of Norman Holmes Pearson	240 letters
Bryher	240 letters
Southern Illinois University	2,539 letters
Aldington, A. E.	1 letter
Aldington, P. A. G.	274 letters
Armstrong	1 letter
Barrow	1 letter
Barton	1 letter
Birch	1 letter
Bonham-Carter	7 letters
Bookishly	1 letter
Browning	1 letter

Burke	1 letter
Cate	1 letter
Cockburn	6 letters
Coghill	1 letter
Collins	4 letters
Drake	6 letters
Durrell	197 letters
Dyson	2 letters
Frere	2 letters
Gilbert	1 letter
Glass	1 letter
Guillaume	1 letter
Hall	1 letter
Hanley	5 letters
Holroyd-Reece	2 letters
Horn and Birkett	1 letter
Hutchens	4 letters
Joynson-Hicks	1 letter
Kershaw, Alister	1,201 letters
Kershaw, Shelia	1 letter
Laughlin	1 letter
Lawrence, Professor	1 letter
Layton	1 letter
Malcolm	1 letter
Miller	1 letter
de Montalk	97 letters
Munson	1 letter
Nethercot	2 letters
Orioli	14 letters
Patmore, Derek	41 letters
Pearce	1 letter
Pinker, J. R.	194 letters
Politzer	6 letters

Dibben	201 letters
Roditi	1 letter
Temple University	81 letters
Aldington, A. E.	20 letters
Aldington, Margery and Patricia	1 letter
Aldington, May	6 letters
Aldington, Miss	1 letter
Aldington, Miss and Mr.	1 letter
Aldington, Patricia	4 letters
Brown	2 letters
Constable	3 letters
Gilbert	38 letters
Mathews	1 letter
Prokosch	1 letter
Sadleir	2 letters
Wright	1 letter
University of Arkansas	9 letters
Fletcher	9 letters
University of Birmingham	1 letter
Young	1 letter
University of Chicago	83 letters
Monroe	79 letters
Rago	3 letters
Udell	1 letter
University of California, Berkeley	9 letters
Parker	9 letters
University of California, Los Angeles	359 letters
Bubb	18 letters
Cate	1 letter
Douglas	1 letter
Manning	2 letters
Manuel	141 letters
Miner	3 letters

Holroyd-Reece	3 letters
Hughes, Babette	10 letters
Hughes, Glenn	46 letters
Hynes	2 letters
Johnson	4 letters
Jonas	2 letters
Kreymbourg	1 letter
Lawrence, Frieda	16 letters
Lehmann	2 letters
Loving	1 letter
Lowell	2 letters
Mackie	1 letter
Monro	1 letter
Morrell	4 letters
Murry	1 letter
Nehls	29 letters
Norman	7 letters
Orioli	8 letters
Palmer	1 letter
Patmore, Brigit	158 letters
Patmore, Derek	6 letters
Pound	1 letter
Ravagli	3 letters
Sitwell	1 letter
Snow	1 letter
Titus	20 letters
Waugh	1 letter
University of Toronto	6 letters
Secker	6 letters
University of Virginia	4 letters
Davis	1 letter
Metcalf and Wilson	1 letter
Tewson	2 letters

Brady   1 letter

9

Index to Letters
by Years

Letters addressed to "editors" or other unidentified
recipients as well as undated letters are not included in
this index; also, because of the format of the Checklist,
it is sometimes impossible to know whether letters covering
a span of years were written in each year. In these cases
they have been arbitrarily included in each year. For
full names of recipients and other information, see the
"Alphabetical Listing."

Lowell

Monro

Plank

<u>1917</u>

Brown

Bubb

Cournos

Flint, F.

Johnson

Lowell

Plank

<u>1918</u>

Beaumont

Brown

Bryher

Bubb

Cournos

Doolittle

Flint, F.

Lowell

Monroe

Moore, T. S.

Plank

Pound

Randall

<u>1919</u>

Brown

Bryher

Bubb

Doolittle

Eliot

Flint, F.

Flint, V.

Johnson

Joyce

Lowell

Mathews

May

Monro

Monroe

Moore, T. S.

Pound

Read

Sanderson

Sitwell

Untermeyer

Wells

Wilkinson

<u>1920</u>

Beaumont

Brown

Doolittle

Dujardin

Eliot

Flint, F.

Flint, V.

Lowell

Manning

Monro

Monroe

Moore, T. S.

Moult

Pound

Sitwell

Untermeyer

Wilkinson

Read

<u>1926</u>

Brown

Fletcher

Gaige

Guerard

Hughes, G.

Monro

Pound

Read

<u>1927</u>

Brown

Covici

Doran

Fletcher

Gaige

Gosse

Hughes, G.

Isaac

Joyce

Monro

Pound

Randall

Read

Slonimsky, H.

Squire

<u>1928</u>

Brown

Fitzgerald

Gaige

Hughes, B.

Hughes, G.

Joyce

Lewis

Monro

Patmore, B.

Patmore, D.

Pound

Putnam

Randall

Slonimsky, H.

<u>1929</u>

Cournos

Cunard

Dobrée

Doolittle

Flanner

Fletcher

Gaige

Glass

Hanley

Hughes, B.

Hughes, G.

Jones

Lewis

Loving

Marshall

Monro

Patmore, B.

Patmore, D.

Pinker, J. R.

Plank

Pound

Read

Sadleir

Slonimsky, H.

Gaige

Lewis

Orioli

Patmore, B.

Patmore, D.

Pinker, J. R.

Pollard

Randall

Read

Reeves

Schiff

Slonimsky, H.

Theis

Warman, E.

Waugh

1934

Cournos

Davis

Doolittle

Dyson

Gilbert

Lewis

Orioli

Patmore, B.

Pinker, J. R.

Plank

Pound

Read

Schiff

Secker

Theis

Van Doren

Warman, E.

1935

Aldington, Patricia

Bacon

Cate

Church

Doolittle

Gilbert

Lewis

Malcolm

Moult

Orioli

Patmore, D.

Schiff

Secker

Slonimksy, H.

1936

Bacon

Coghill

Doolittle

Evans, C. S.

Gilbert

Lewis

Munson

Orioli

Patmore, D.

Read

Schiff

Warman, E.

Wells

1937

Bacon

Doolittle

Evans, C. S.

Slonimsky, H.

Warman, E.

<u>1943</u>

Bacon

Best

Manuel

Slonimsky, H.

Slonimsky, M.

Strassman

Warman, E.

<u>1944</u>

Arlott

Bacon

Best

Manuel

Powell

Slonimsky, H.

Warman, E.

<u>1945</u>

Aldington, P. A. G.

Bacon

Best

Doolittle

Manuel

Powell

Slonimsky, H.

Warman, E.

<u>1946</u>

Aldington, P. A. G.

Bacon

Church

Covici

Doolittle

Frere

Manuel

Powell

Read

Slonimsky, H.

Warman, E.

<u>1947</u>

Aldington, P. A. G.

Bacon

Best

Dibben

Doolittle

Frere

Kershaw, A.

Manuel

Powell

Slonimsky, H.

Snow

Warman, E.

<u>1948</u>

Aldington, P. A. G.

Bacon

Callender

Covici

Dibben

Doolittle

Frere

Hall

Harding-Edgar

Kershaw, A.

Manuel

Miller

Powell

Miner

Pound

Russell

Slonimsky, M.

Van Patten

1952

Aldington, Netta

Aldington, P. A. G.

Bird

Collins

Covici

Deasey

Dibben

Doolittle

Frere

Holroyd-Reece

Kershaw, A.

Langham

Manuel

Megata

Nehls

Pound

Prentice

Rappaport

Russell

Slonimsky, H.

Slonimsky, M.

Taylor

Warman, E.

1953

Aldington, Netta

Aldington, P. A. G.

Bacon

Bird

Bryher

Campbell, R.

Collins

Covici

Deasey

Dibben

Doolittle

Frere

Holroyd-Reece

Hutchens

Kershaw, A.

Manuel

Megata

Morris

Nehls

Politzer

Pound

Randall

Rappaport

Secker

Slonimsky, M.

Warman, E.

1954

Aldington, Netta

Aldington, P. A. G.

Bacon

Bird

Bonham-Carter

Bryher

Campbell

Church

Cockburn

Aldington, Netta

Aldington, P. A. G.

Bird

Bonham-Carter

Bryher

Campbell, R.

Dahlberg

Deasey

Dibben

Doolittle

Dutton

Evans, A.

Frere

Guillaume

Harrison

Kershaw, A.

Lawrence, F.

Lyle

Manuel

Megata

de Montalk

Nehls

Noble

Parker

Pound

Rago

Randall

Rappaport

Ravagli

Read

Russell

Temple

Thompson

Urnov

Walters

Warman, E.

1957

Aldington, Netta

Aldington, P. A. G.

Atkins

Berkhoff

Bird

Bonham-Carter

Bryher

Deasey

Doolittle

Durrell

Dutton

Frere

Harrison

Horn & Birkett

Kershaw, A.

de Montalk

Nehls

Parker

Pound

Rago

Randall

Rankin

Rappaport

Read

Temple

Urnov

Walters

Warman, E.

Zhantieva

Aldington, P. A. G.

Aldington, Patricia

Barnes

Bird

Bryher

Deasey

Doolittle

Durrell

Dutton

Frere

Gilbert

Harald, M.

Kershaw, A.

Megata

de Montalk

Moore, H. T.

Norman

Parker

Pound

Powell

Randall

Sternberg

Temple

Urnov

Vincendon

Warman, E.

Zhantieva

1961

Aldington, Netta

Aldington, P. A. G.

Aldington, Patricia

Armstrong

Bird

Bryher

Covici

Doolittle

Durrell

Dutton

Gilbert

Gribble, Guy

Harald, Mrs.

Kershaw, A.

Machin

Megata

de Montalk

Moore, H. T.

Norman

Pearson

Powell

Randall

Read

Sternberg

Temple

Urnov

Vincendon

Warman, E.

Zhantieva

1962

Aldington, Netta

Aldington, P. A. G.

Armstrong

Bird

Bryher

Covici

Durrell

Dutton